Collins

Student Support
Materials for AQA

A-level Year 2
Biology

Topics 5 and 6: Energy transfers in and between organisms, Organisms respond to changes in their internal and external environment

Author: Mike Boyle

William Collins' dream of knowledge for all began with the publication of his first book in 1819.

A self-educated mill worker, he not only enriched millions of lives, but also founded a flourishing publishing house. Today, staying true to this spirit, Collins books are packed with inspiration, innovation and practical expertise. They place you at the centre of a world of possibility and give you exactly what you need to explore it.

Collins. Freedom to teach

HarperCollins Publishers
The News Building
1 London Bridge Street
London SE1 9GF

> **Browse the complete Collins catalogue at**
> **www.collins.co.uk**

10 9 8 7 6 5 4 3 2 1

© HarperCollins*Publishers* 2016

ISBN 978-0-00-818947-1

Collins® is a registered trademark of HarperCollins*Publishers* Limited

www.collins.co.uk

A catalogue record for this book is available from the British Library

Commissioned by Gillian Lindsey
Edited by Alexander Rutherford
Project managed by Maheswari PonSaravanan at Jouve
Development by Kate Redmond and Gillian Lindsey
Copyedited by Rebecca Ramsden
Proof read by Janette Schubert
Original design by Newgen Imaging
Typeset by Jouve India Private Limited
Cover design by Angela English
Printed by CPI Group (UK) Ltd, Croydon, CR0 4YY
Cover image © iStock/royaltystockphoto

Contents

3.5 Energy transfers in and between organisms

3.5.1 Photosynthesis

Notes

The different pigments in chlorophyll are commonly separated by paper chromatography, and the pigments identified by calculating their R_f **value**.

Essential Notes

NADPH is similar to NADH (seen in respiration, section 3.5.2) and performs basically the same electron-carrying function. It is useful to remember 'P for photosynthesis'; NADH in respiration, NADPH in photosynthesis.
(**NB**: in reality, the 'P' stands for phosphate.)

Notes

A common mistake is to state that starch in a chloroplast provides extra energy for photosynthesis.

Photosynthesis is often seen by students as a difficult topic to learn, but you can make sense of it all if you approach it in the right way. First, you need an overview; this provides a framework on which you can fit the details. The best way to start is to divide photosynthesis into two easy steps.

1 **The light-dependent reaction** – light hits **chlorophyll**, which then emits high-energy electrons (**photoionisation**). These electrons pass through a series of electron transfer reactions that make **ATP** (adenosine triphosphate) and **reduced NADP** (also called NADPH). The electrons in chlorophyll are replaced when water is split, a process that also produces oxygen as a by-product.

2 **The light-independent reaction** – ATP and reduced NADP are used in a series of reactions known as the **Calvin cycle** (Fig 2). Overall, these reactions **reduce** carbon dioxide to glucose.

Both steps take place in the **chloroplast** (Fig 1), but it is important to remember that different reactions happen in different parts of this important organelle.

The light-dependent reaction

The light-dependent reaction can be outlined as follows:

● This process happens on the **thylakoids**, which are membranes within the chloroplast that contain the chlorophyll molecules.

● When a photon of light hits a molecule of chlorophyll, the pigment becomes *excited* (raised to a higher energy level) and emits two high-energy electrons.

● These excited electrons pass down an **electron transfer chain** on the thylakoid membrane. The result is ATP synthesis by **photophosphorylation**.

Fig 1
Chloroplasts are organelles that house all the enzymes and other substances needed for photosynthesis; they take the form of biconvex discs (rather like Smarties™ – but don't call them that in the examination).

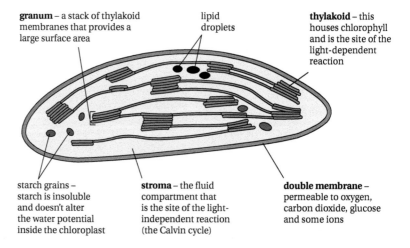

granum – a stack of thylakoid membranes that provides a large surface area

lipid droplets

thylakoid – this houses chlorophyll and is the site of the light-dependent reaction

starch grains – starch is insoluble and doesn't alter the water potential inside the chloroplast

stroma – the fluid compartment that is the site of the light-independent reaction (the Calvin cycle)

double membrane – permeable to oxygen, carbon dioxide, glucose and some ions

- Energy is also used to split water via the process of **photolysis**, which produces new electrons to replace those lost by the chlorophyll. Protons (hydrogen ions) and oxygen are made as by-products.

- Electrons are used to make reduced NADP.

- ATP and reduced NADP are essential for the light-independent reaction, and oxygen is released into the atmosphere.

The synthesis of ATP

ATP synthase is a large enzyme that is found embedded in the inner membranes of both mitochondria (cristae) and chloroplasts (thylakoids). In both cases the molecule is very similar in structure and is driven by a flow of H^+ ions (protons) through the centre of the molecule. Protons carry a positive charge, so whenever there is an unequal distribution there will be an electrochemical gradient: a difference in both concentration and charge.

The movement of protons down an electrochemical gradient is called **chemiosmosis**. The proton movement makes part of the ATP synthase enzyme rotate, and in doing so it catalyses the synthesis of ATP from ADP and inorganic phosphate (Pi).

- In the electron transfer chain at the end of respiration this process is called **oxidative phosphorylation**.

- In the light-dependent reaction of photosynthesis this process is called **photophosphorylation**.

The light-independent reaction

The light-independent reaction can be outlined as follows:

- This process happens in the **stroma**, the fluid in the centre of the chloroplast.

- It involves the reduction of carbon dioxide by a series of reactions known as the Calvin cycle. The essential stages of this cycle are shown in Fig 2.

Essential Notes

The general term ATPase is often used to describe any enzyme that interacts with ATP but it is more useful and accurate to use:

- ATP synthase – makes ATP from ADP and an inorganic phosphate group

- ATP hydrolase – splits ATP into ADP and an inorganic phosphate group

ATP is hydrolysed in many different processes. Three important examples are muscular contraction (see section 3.6.3), active transport (covered in year 1) and protein synthesis (covered in year 1).

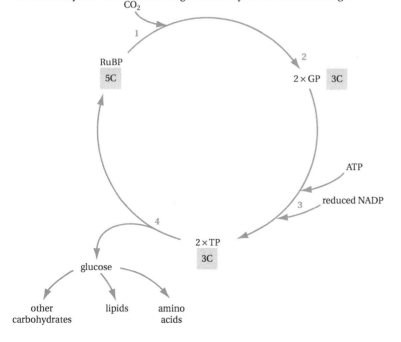

Fig 2
The Calvin cycle. The number of carbon atoms in each molecule is shown in the shaded squares next to the molecule it refers to.

- ATP and reduced NADP are used to reduce the carbon dioxide. Supplies of these compounds depend on light, so, when it gets dark, the light-independent reaction finishes soon after the light-dependent reaction.

The four key stages of the Calvin cycle can be described as follows:

1 Carbon dioxide combines with the 5-carbon compound **ribulose bisphosphate (RuBP)**. This reaction is catalysed by the enzyme **rubisco** (ribulose bisphosphate carboxylase).

2 This produces a highly unstable 6-carbon compound that immediately splits into two molecules of **glycerate 3-phosphate (GP**, a 3-carbon compound).

3 ATP and reduced NADP are used to reduce the GP into **triose phosphate (TP**, another 3-carbon compound), sometimes referred to as GALP (glyceraldehyde phosphate). This is the first compound that is actually a sugar.

4 Some of the triose phosphate is used to make carbohydrate, but most of it is used to make more RuBP to continue the cycle. For every glucose molecule produced, five molecules of RuBP are re-synthesised. Glucose can be converted into many other essential organic compounds. As well as the comparatively simple conversion into starch, glucose can also be converted into triglycerides and, using phosphate and nitrate ions from the soil, phospholipids, proteins and nucleic acids.

Essential Notes

TP (triose phosphate) is sometimes referred to as GALP (glyceraldehyde phosphate).

Essential Notes

The term *triose* simply means a three-carbon sugar.

Limiting factors in photosynthesis

The limiting factor is the one in shortest supply. Increase the supply and you will increase the rate of reaction. Common limiting factors of photosynthesis include temperature, carbon dioxide concentration and light intensity. For example, at night, light is obviously a limiting factor. At dawn, the light intensity increases and so does the rate of photosynthesis until some other factor – possibly carbon dioxide level – becomes limiting.

Temperature is often a limiting factor. The light-dependent reaction is not particularly temperature sensitive because it doesn't rely on enzymes. Instead, it relies on the excitation of chlorophyll followed by electron transfer chains. In contrast, the light-independent reaction is much more temperature dependent because it is controlled by enzymes.

A knowledge of limiting factors and how to increase their supply is obviously important in agriculture (Table 1).

Table 1
Improving the abiotic environment of crop plants

Factor	How supply can be increased	Is it worth it ...	
		in a glasshouse?	in a field?
Temperature	Heater	Possibly	No
Carbon dioxide	Heater – burn a fossil fuel (for example, propane)	Possibly	No
Mineral ions	Add fertiliser	Usually	Usually
Light	Artificial lighting	Possibly	Rarely
Water	Spray or irrigate	Essential	Yes, if rainfall/ irrigation is insufficient

Measuring photosynthesis

A common way to measure the rate of photosynthesis is to use an aquatic plant such as *Elodea* or *Cabomba*, and measure the rate of oxygen consumption. The plant will produce bubbles of oxygen which can be collected (Fig 3).

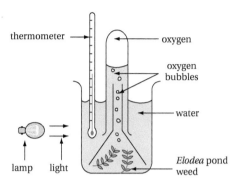

Fig 3
Apparatus used to measure the rate of photosynthesis in *Elodea* pond weed

This apparatus can be used to investigate the effect of various environmental factors. Light intensity, temperature and hydrogencarbonate (dissolved CO_2) concentration can all be used as independent variables. A common problem is the need to perform repeat experiments, given that no two pieces of pond weed will be identical. To allow differently-sized specimens to be compared, the surface area of each plant used can be estimated (which is messy, and usually involves each leaf being removed and its area estimated using graph paper). This allows the rate of photosynthesis to be given as 'volume of oxygen per unit time per unit surface area of leaf'. For example, $5\,cm^3\,O_2\,min^{-1}\,cm^{-2}$.

Are we really measuring the rate of photosynthesis?

The simple answer is 'no', because we haven't taken **respiration** into account. The amount of oxygen a plant gives off is a measure of how much the rate of photosynthesis *exceeds* the rate of respiration. The actual rate of photosynthesis can be estimated if the experiment is repeated in the dark.

For example, a student measured the rate of photosynthesis in the light and the rate of respiration in the dark (Table 2).

Process	Volume of oxygen used or made (cm^3) per minute
Respiration in dark	3 used
Rate of photosynthesis in light	14 made
True rate of photosynthesis	17

Table 2
Results of experiment to measure the rate of photosynthesis in the light and rate of respiration in the dark

Investigating the effect of a named factor on the rate of dehydrogenase activity in extracts of chloroplasts

The basic theory behind an investigation into the rate of dehydrogenase activity in extracts of chloroplasts is that during the light-dependent reaction, NADP acts as an electron acceptor and so becomes reduced in the process: it becomes reduced NADP. The reaction is catalysed by a **dehydrogenase** enzyme, that catalyses the removal of hydrogen. In this investigation a different electron acceptor, DCPIP, is used. This is a redox indicator. It is a blue colour in its oxidised form, and turns colourless when it accepts an electron, i.e. when it is reduced.

If you add DCPIP to a suspension of isolated chloroplast in the light, it will quickly lose its blue colour because it is reduced by the electrons emitted by the excited chlorophyll. If you do this in the dark, the blue colour remains.

This method can be used to investigate the effect of different wavelengths of light, or of different light intensities or temperatures. The faster the rate of the light-dependent reaction, the faster the blue colour disappears.

3.5.2 Respiration

Notes

Be careful how you use the term 'energy'. The process of respiration releases the energy in organic molecules, and transfers it to ATP. Candidates often lose marks when they state that respiration makes or produces energy. Energy cannot be made or destroyed.

Notes

Students often lose marks by stating that ATP is needed *for* respiration. Respiration takes energy from organic molecules and uses it to *make* ATP.

Respiration is the release of energy from organic molecules. In this section, we study the breakdown of glucose. This is the main fuel for respiration in humans, but many other organic compounds can also be respired. For example, we respire lipids when our carbohydrate stores run low, and many carnivorous animals, such as cats, get much of their energy by respiring amino acids from their high-protein diet.

In practice, full **aerobic respiration** consists of four processes. These are shown in Fig 4, and are described below.

1   **Glycolysis** – one molecule of glucose is split into two molecules of **pyruvate**.

2   **Link reaction** – pyruvate is converted into **acetate**, which then combines with **co-enzyme A** (or **CoA**) to become **acetyl co-enzyme A** (often shortened to **acetyl CoA**).

3   **Krebs cycle** – electrons are removed from the acetyl CoA.

4   **Electron transfer chain** – the energy in the electrons is used to make large amounts of ATP.

Respiration is an energy-releasing process that takes place in virtually *all* living cells *all* of the time. In order to understand respiration, you need to know about the co-enzyme, **NAD**.

What is NAD?

NAD stands for nicotinamide adenine dinucleotide; although you will not be asked to remember the full name. NAD is a **co-enzyme** and its key feature is that it carries electrons.

$$NAD^+ + e^- \rightarrow \text{reduced NAD (NADH)}$$

co-enzyme + electron $\rightarrow$ reduced co-enzyme

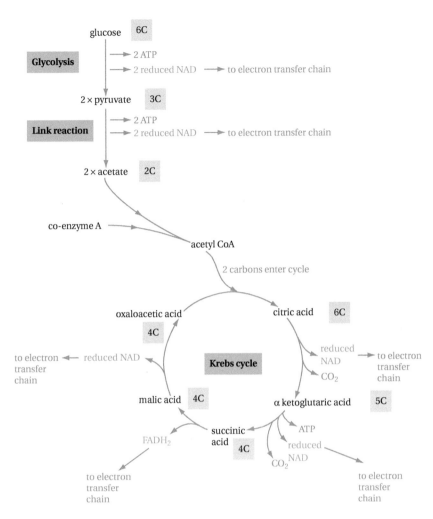

Fig 4
An overview of respiration showing glycolysis, the link reaction, the Krebs cycle and the electron transfer chain. The number of carbon atoms in each molecule is shown in the shaded squares next to the molecule it refers to.

Electron transfer chain:

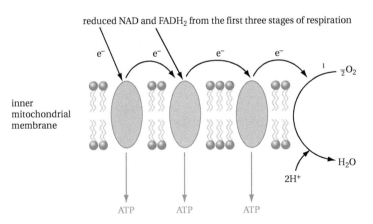

Respiration is basically a series of **oxidation** reactions that remove electrons from the original organic molecule. These electrons are picked up by NAD, forming **reduced NADH**, also called NADH. So whenever you see NADH, think: 'an electron is being carried'.

NADH carries electrons into the electron transfer system, where they are used to make large amounts of ATP. $FADH_2$, made in the Krebs cycle, is similar to NADH and has exactly the same electron-carrying function.

The location of each respiration reaction in a **mitochondrion** is shown in Fig 5.

Fig 5
What-happens-where in a
mitochondrion

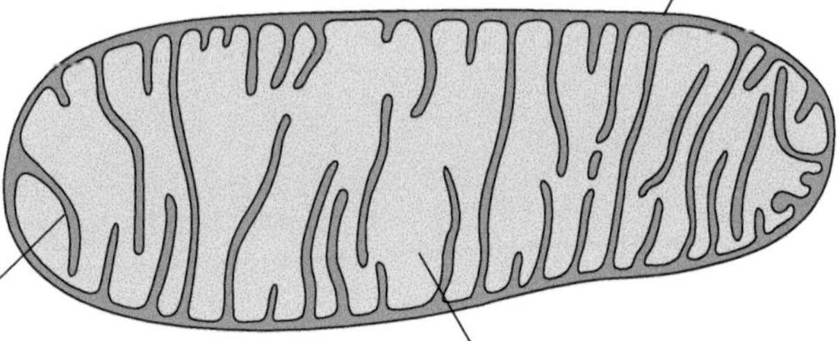

glycolysis takes place outside the mitochondrion; when glucose has been oxidised to pyruvate, this passes into the matrix to complete the aerobic parts of respiration

outer membrane

cristae – folds of the inner membrane; these provide a large surface area for the reactions of the *electron transfer chain*

matrix – the inner fluid of the mitochondrion where the *link reaction* and the *Krebs cycle* take place

Essential Notes

Note the similarities in the structure of a chloroplast and a mitochondrion (Fig 1 and Fig 5). Both are about the same size (roughly 10 µm across) and both have an internal membrane system giving a large surface area for reactions. Both convert energy: chloroplasts convert light energy into chemical energy (by making glucose, etc.); while mitochondria convert one form of chemical energy (glucose, etc.) into another (ATP). Both make ATP via chemiosmosis and ATP synthase enzymes embedded in their inner membranes.

Each of the four reactions of respiration (shown in italics in Fig 5) are looked at in detail below.

Glycolysis

- The word glycolysis means 'sugar splitting'.

- In glycolysis, one molecule of glucose (a 6-carbon compound) is oxidised to produce two molecules of pyruvate (a 3-carbon compound).

- The reaction yields two molecules of ATP and two molecules of reduced NAD (NADH) for each glucose molecule that is split. (It actually uses two ATP molecules but produces four – a net profit of two.)

- Glycolysis takes place in the **cytosol** – the fluid part of the cytoplasm (*not* in the mitochondria).

- The process does not require oxygen. **Anaerobic respiration** is basically just glycolysis.

A key idea in glycolysis is that glucose is first raised to a higher energy level, making it more reactive, which is done by adding two phosphate groups. Once it has been phosphorylated, it is split into two molecules of triose phosphate. This uses two molecules of ATP. Finally, triose phosphate is oxidised into pyruvate. For each original glucose molecule we make two molecules of ATP (two were used but four were made), two of reduced NAD (NADH) and two of pyruvate.

In eukaryotic cells, and if oxygen is available, pyruvate then enters the mitochondria and is used to fuel the rest of the reactions of aerobic respiration.

Link reaction

This reaction is so named because it links glycolysis to the Krebs cycle.

- This reaction is also called pyruvate oxidation.

- In the link reaction, pyruvate is used to produce acetate and carbon dioxide. The acetate is picked up by co-enzyme A, forming acetyl co-enzyme A.

- No ATP is produced during the link reaction, but two molecules of reduced NAD (NADH) are formed.

- The link reaction takes place in the **matrix** (inner fluid) of the mitochondria (see Fig 5).

Krebs cycle

- This cycle is a series of reactions that oxidise what is left of the glucose after it has passed through glycolysis and the link reaction. By now, the glucose has been converted to acetate. In the Krebs cycle electrons are stripped from the acetate, creating large amounts of the electron carriers NADH and $FADH_2$.

- The reactions take place in the matrix of the mitochondria.

- Each turn of the cycle produces one ATP, three NADH, one $FADH_2$ and two CO_2 molecules.

- The cycle turns twice per molecule of glucose. It therefore produces two ATP, six NADH, two $FADH_2$ and four CO_2 molecules per molecule of glucose.

The electron transfer chain

- This consists of a series of carrier proteins on the inner mitochondrial membrane, which is folded into **cristae** to provide a large surface area for the process.

- Electrons are delivered to the electron transfer chain by NADH and $FADH_2$.

- The electrons pass from one protein to the next along the chain.

- Each electron transfer is an oxidation/reduction reaction that releases energy.

- This energy is used to pump protons (H^+ ions) from the matrix, across the inner membrane into the outer mitochondrial space by **active transport**.

- This creates a concentration gradient of H^+ ions, which diffuse back into the mitochondrial matrix through the centre of molecules of ATP synthase enzymes (see Fig 6). As they do so, the ATP synthase enzyme catalyses the synthesis of a molecule of ATP.

- The by-products of this process are low-energy electrons and protons, which combine with oxygen to form water.

- You are breathing at this moment because of the electron transfer chain. You need to provide oxygen to mop up the electrons, and also to remove the accumulated carbon dioxide from your lungs.

Essential Notes

Respiration and photosynthesis both consist of a series of steps. Each step is a relatively simple chemical reaction that is controlled by a specific enzyme.

Essential Notes

Reduced enzymes can be thought of as credit notes that can be cashed in during the electron transfer chain.

Each NADH can be cashed in for three ATPs, and each $FADH_2$ can be cashed in for two ATPs.

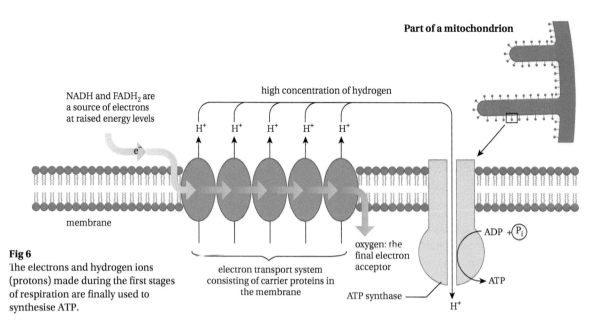

Part of a mitochondrion

NADH and FADH$_2$ are a source of electrons at raised energy levels

high concentration of hydrogen

H$^+$ H$^+$ H$^+$ H$^+$ H$^+$

e$^-$

membrane

electron transport system consisting of carrier proteins in the membrane

oxygen: the final electron acceptor

ATP synthase

ADP + P$_i$

ATP

H$^+$

Fig 6
The electrons and hydrogen ions (protons) made during the first stages of respiration are finally used to synthesise ATP.

How much ATP is made per glucose molecule?

In ideal conditions the theoretical maximum is 38 molecules. Below we see why.

There are two ways of making ATP:

- **Substrate level phosphorylation** – the method of ATP production in glycolysis and the Krebs cycle. Both processes provide two ATP molecules per glucose, giving a total of four ATP molecules by this method.

- By **oxidative phosphorylation** – here, ATP is made using energy released in the electron transfer system. In effect, it is ATP made by 'cashing in' the energy in the electrons carried by NADH and FADH$_2$. The other 34 molecules of ATP made during respiration per molecule of glucose are made by this method (see below).

Table 3
The total ATP and NADH production from the first three parts of respiration, per molecule of glucose

Process	ATP made	NADH made	FADH$_2$ made
Glycolysis	2	2	0
Link reaction	0	2	0
Krebs cycle	2	6	2
Totals	4	10	2

When fed into the electron transfer chain, three ATP molecules are made per NADH, and two per FADH$_2$. This gives us:

From NADH: $10 \times 3 = 30$ ATP

From FADH$_2$: $2 \times 2 = 4$ ATP

This gives a total of 34 molecules of ATP made by oxidative phosphorylation. When we add these to the original four produced by glycolysis and the Krebs cycle, we get the 38 ATPs produced per molecule of glucose during aerobic respiration. In practice, slightly fewer ATP molecules are made, for a variety of complex reasons.

Anaerobic respiration

This is respiration without oxygen, and it's a much simpler process than aerobic respiration. It's basically glycolysis that doesn't go any further. Compared to aerobic respiration, anaerobic respiration:

- produces less ATP (two compared to about 38)
- takes place in the cytoplasm, not in the mitochondria
- only takes a short time to complete.

In all organisms, glucose is converted into pyruvate. As a general guide, animals and bacteria convert pyruvate into **lactate**, while plants and fungi convert the pyruvate into carbon dioxide and **ethanol**.

In both cases, the conversion of pyruvate is essential because it re-synthesises NAD^+ from NADH. This is vital because otherwise there would be no more NAD^+ available and so glycolysis could not continue.

Measuring respiration

How do you measure the rate of respiration? You can measure energy production (as heat) or oxygen consumption, but in practice the latter is easier. Fig 7 shows one type of respirometer.

A respirometer works in the following way:

- The organism respires. It takes in oxygen and gives out carbon dioxide.
- Normally, this will not change the volume of the gas in the apparatus, because the carbon dioxide made will replace the oxygen used.
- But, the sodium hydroxide absorbs all of the carbon dioxide, so it's just as if the organism isn't making any carbon dioxide.
- As a result, the volume of the air in the chamber decreases as the organism uses oxygen. This draws the fluid along the tube and the rate of oxygen used per unit time can be measured.
- Suitable units for rate of respiration will include the volume of oxygen used per unit mass of the organism per unit time. Actual units will depend on the timescale and the size of the organism. For example, cubic centimetres of oxygen per gram per hour ($cm^3 O_2 \, g^{-1} h^{-1}$).

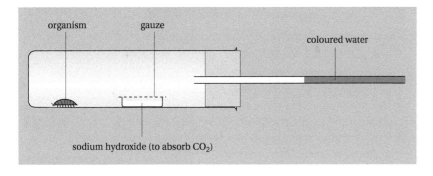

Fig 7
A simple respirometer

3.5.3 Energy and ecosystems

The importance of photosynthesis

Photosynthesis is the only process that can capture sunlight energy and so it is the major route by which energy enters an **ecosystem**. In photosynthesis, sunlight is used to reduce carbon dioxide into organic molecules. Initially, simple carbohydrates (sugars) are made, but plants can make other molecules such as lipids, proteins and nucleic acid, by modifying the carbohydrates. In this way, plants make the food molecules that support whole ecosystems. The by-product of photosynthesis is oxygen – another substance vital to life on Earth. Organisms that can photosynthesise are called **producers**. The relationship between producers and other types of organisms in an ecosystem is shown in Table 5.

Table 4
The relationship between producers, decomposers and consumers

Type of organism	What it needs	What it produces
Producer (green plants and algae)	Carbon dioxide, inorganic ions	Oxygen, organic molecules
Consumer (mainly animals)	Organic molecules, oxygen	Carbon dioxide, organic waste
Decomposer (bacteria and fungi)	Organic molecules, oxygen	Carbon dioxide, inorganic ions (nitrate, etc.)*

* Only bacteria produce inorganic ions

Where does the energy from sunlight go?

A huge amount of solar energy reaches our planet but only a small percentage is captured by plants in photosynthesis and packaged into organic molecules (biomass). The rest of the energy is lost in different ways.

- A large amount of sunlight misses plants altogether – some of it heats the atmosphere; some of it heats the seas and rocks.

- Not all the light that reaches a plant hits the chloroplasts – some passes straight through the plant, or is reflected.

- Some light is of the wrong wavelength – plants use mainly the blue and red light in the visible spectrum, and reflect green. Some energy is used in the evaporation of water from the leaves (transpiration).

- The reactions of photosynthesis, like all reactions, are inefficient – some energy is always transferred to the surroundings as heat.

- The term **gross primary production (GPP)** refers to the total chemical energy store in the organic molecules produced by a plant. However, the plant uses a proportion of the energy store for its own needs – this energy is released when the plant respires or dies and decomposes. Only the surplus energy produced by the plant – the **net primary production (NPP)** – is available to the rest of the ecosystem.

- Put as an equation:

$$NPP = GPP - R \text{ (where } R = \text{respiration)}$$

Notes

You could be asked to calculate any of the following (with units, see below):
- NPP, which is GPP – R
- GPP, which is NPP + R
- R, which is GPP – NPP.

Fig 8 shows the energy transfer along an Antarctic food chain. The Sun may send us a large amount of energy but the transfer of energy at each level is very inefficient (see page 18).

Fig 9 shows one way to illustrate the different ways in which energy transferred to a consumer (the chemical energy stored in ingested food) is lost to the environment.

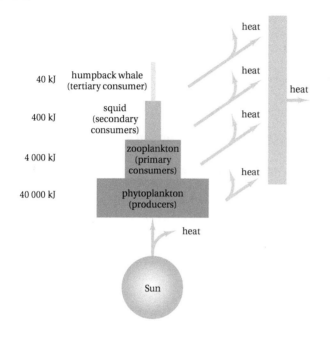

Fig 8
The energy transfer for an Antarctic food chain showing the percentage energy transfer at each level; at each stage, over 90% of the available energy is transferred to the surroundings as heat

Notes

Make sure you are clear about how energy is lost. It's basic thermodynamics: energy transfers are never 100% efficient and some is always lost as heat. Movement, for example, involves two energy transfers – from glucose to ATP in respiration and from ATP to kinetic energy in muscular contraction – so there are two opportunities to lose heat.

Invertebrate herbivore

Invertebrate carnivore

Mammal herbivore

Mammal carnivore

Fig 9
Energy transfer boxes for four animals
T = total energy in the food eaten
  NB: food that cannot be digested cannot be absorbed, and so is not available to the organism
A = energy absorbed
F = energy lost in faeces
R = energy lost in respiration
P = energy incorporated into the tissues of the organism; this is the energy passed on to the next **trophic level**

Note two important trends:
1 Mammals pass a smaller proportion of their energy intake up the food chain because they use more energy to maintain their body temperature
2 Carnivores are more efficient at converting their food into body tissue because meat has less indigestible material than plant-based food

Biomass

Biomass refers to the total mass of the living (or recently living) tissue. Biomass usually refers to a particular population within the ecosystem, but can also refer to a trophic level within the ecosystem (such as all the plant biomass in a field). Biomass can be measured in terms of mass of carbon or dry mass (once all the water has been removed) of tissue per given area per given time. For example, kg m-2 day-1, which is kilogrammes per square metre per day.

Units of GPP

The units of GPP are kJ per given area or volume, in a given time. Area (or volume, e.g. for aquatic algae) and time must be taken into consideration, otherwise you can't compare different ecosystems or crops, or the same ecosystem/crop at different times. The exact units vary according to scale, but a typical one would be $kJ\ m^{-2}\ day^{-1}$, which is kilojoules per square metre per day.

Estimating the chemical energy store in dry biomass using calorimetry

The chemical energy store in dry biomass can be estimated using calorimetry. The basic idea is that a sample is first dried and then burned in oxygen in a sealed container (sometimes called the 'bomb', Fig 10), and the energy given off is used to heat water. The energy content can be calculated from the **specific heat capacity** of water: 4.2 J of energy is required to raise the temperature of 1 g of water by 1°C ($4.2\ g^{-1}\ °C$).

Calorimetry – sample calculation

A chicken nugget weighing 17.5 g was burned in oxygen in a bomb calorimeter. It raised the temperature of 1000 cm^3 of water by 40 °C.

Calculate the energy content per gram of chicken nugget.

$$\text{energy transferred (in J)} = \frac{\text{change in temperature (in °C)}}{\text{mass (in g)} \times \text{specific heat capacity (in } g^{-1}\ °C^{-1})}$$

The specific heat capacity of water is 4.2 J $g^{-1}\ °C^{-1}$

$$\text{energy transferred} = 1000 \times 4.2 \times 40$$

$$= 168\ 000\ \text{J or } 168\ \text{kJ}$$

$$\text{energy transferred per gram} = \frac{168\ \text{kJ}}{17.5\ \text{g}} = 9.6\ \text{kJ g}^{-1}$$

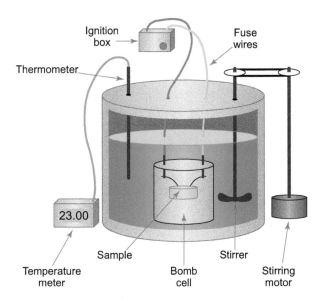

Fig 10
A bomb calorimeter

Calculating the energy efficiency of energy transfers within ecosystems

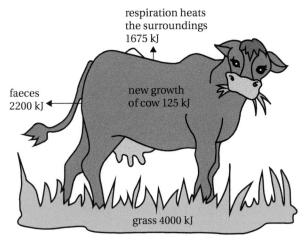

Fig 11
Calculating the efficiency of a grazing animal

The basic question is: how much of the energy stored in the plants/producers goes into the tissues of the animals that eat them? Fig 11 shows the results of an investigation into the efficiency of one individual cow.

The animal is given grass storing a known amount of chemical energy. This would be worked out by calorimetry, as described above. A large proportion of the dry mass of the grass is cellulose, which is difficult to digest. Despite having gut microbes that help to digest the cellulose, a lot of energy stored in the food is lost in the faeces.

- The energy stored in the food eaten was 4000 kJ.

- Some unfortunate individual had the job of collecting, drying and working out the energy content of the faeces by calorimetry. The energy store in the dry faeces was 2200 kJ so we can assume that 1800 kJ was transferred into the bloodstream. This is the energy available to the organism.

- Of the energy in the food that was digested and absorbed, 1675 kJ was lost to the environment as heat. This figure is always high in endotherms (warm-blooded animals).

- So just 125 kJ was incorporated into the tissues of the animal. This is what is available to the next trophic level. You might like to think of this as the energy in meat, but the animal also makes less digestible (and profitable) tissue such as bone and skin.

- The efficiency of energy transfer is calculated from 125 kJ as a percentage of 4000 kJ, which is 3.125%

Efficiency of energy transfers at different trophic levels

Generally speaking, the energy transfer from the Sun to the producers is the least efficient, for the reasons outlined above. A typical value would be about 1% but this varies according to the type of producer and the environmental conditions. The efficiency of the energy transfer from producer to primary consumer is typically 2–5%. The transfer from animal to animal is generally more efficient, often in the region of 5–10%. One reason for this is that animal tissue ('meat') is more digestible than plant matter and so less energy is lost in faeces.

From this we can see that most of the available energy is lost at each trophic level and so the more steps there are in the chain, the less energy there is for the organisms at the top. There are usually three steps in a chain; rarely more than five. The number of steps in a food chain is always limited because there is no energy left. In terms of agriculture, it is much more efficient to grow plants than it is to produce meat.

3.5.4 Nutrient cycles

Essential Notes

Bacteria and fungi used to be referred to as **saprophytes** but now the term **saprobionts** is preferred. The terms mean the same thing – decomposers.

Organisms are made from 'secondhand' material. The atoms and molecules that make up your body have been part of many organisms before you, and will probably be part of many different organisms long after you are gone. These resources are finite, and are recycled again and again. Importantly, energy is not recycled – we need a continued supply in order to drive the cycles, building up simple molecules into more complex molecules and then breaking them down again. You need to know about the **phosphorus cycle** and the **nitrogen cycle**.

The role of microorganisms

As we shall see below, microorganisms play a vital role in recycling chemical elements, either as **saprobionts** in decomposition or in nitrification and denitrification. Microorganisms are also important in facilitating the uptake of water and inorganic ions, such as phosphorus and nitrogen, by plants.

The word **mycorrhizae** means 'fungus root'. It has been found, relatively recently, that many plant species live in association with a fungus that grows in and around their roots. This association is **mutualistic** – both species benefit – because

- the plant gets a greater surface area for absorbing water and mineral ions
- the fungus gets some of the sugars and other organic compounds made by the plant in photosynthesis.

The nitrogen cycle

Nitrogen is an essential component of several vital compounds including proteins, nucleic acids (RNA and DNA) and ATP. The nitrogen cycle is summarised below and is illustrated in Figs 12 and 13.

- Plants in general absorb nitrogen as nitrate (NO_3^-); a soluble ion that their roots can take in by active transport.
- Plants combine nitrate with the carbohydrate made in photosynthesis to make amino acids and nucleotides, the building blocks of proteins and nucleic acids.
- Nitrogen is passed up the food chain in these large organic molecules when animals eat the plants.
- Finally, all nitrogen ends up in non-living organic material. This could be dead leaves, dead bodies, faeces or urine (which contains nitrogen in urea or uric acid).
- The nitrogen-rich dead matter (**humus** or **detritus**) is broken down by saprobionts, which are bacteria and fungi. These organisms obtain their nutrients by **extracellular digestion** (secretion of enzymes and absorption of the soluble products, such as amino acids). The saprobionts excrete ammonium compounds (NH_4^+ ions).
- The last stage of **saprobiotic nutrition** (production of ammonium compounds from amino acids or other compounds) is **ammonification**.
- The ammonium ions are used by **nitrifying bacteria**. These organisms obtain their energy from oxidation reactions rather than from the Sun; the bacteria obtain their energy from the oxidation of the ammonium ions. This is called **nitrification**.

Notes

Be careful to distinguish between the element nitrogen contained in compounds such as nitrates and protein, and nitrogen in the atmosphere. When referring to atmospheric nitrogen always write 'nitrogen gas'.

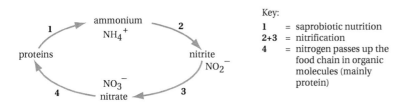

Key:
1 = saprobiotic nutrition
2+3 = nitrification
4 = nitrogen passes up the food chain in organic molecules (mainly protein)

Fig 12
The nitrogen cycle

Notes

Learn the basic nitrogen cycle, as shown in Fig 12, before you attempt to learn all its complications.

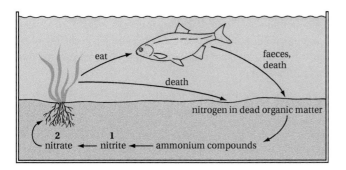

Fig 13
The nitrogen cycle in a fish tank

Essential Notes

You won't be expected to recall the names of the different types of bacteria involved in nitrification, though this level of extra detail can be useful in synoptic essays.

Notes

Make sure that you can distinguish between:

- nitrifying bacteria that turn ammonium into nitrates – 'the good guys'
- denitrifying bacteria that turn nitrates into nitrogen gas – 'the bad guys'
- nitrogen-fixing bacteria that turn nitrogen gas into ammonia – 'the angels'.

Nitrification

Nitrification is a two-stage process, as indicated by the numbers (1 and 2) in Fig 13, which shows the nitrogen cycle in a fish tank:

1 The ammonium ions are oxidised into nitrite (NO_2^-) ions by bacteria of the genus *Nitrosomonas*.

2 The nitrite is further oxidised into nitrate (NO_3^-) ions by bacteria of the genus *Nitrobacter*.

Finally, the soluble nitrate is absorbed by plants and the cycle repeats itself.

As well as the main cycle described above, you also need to know how nitrogen can be lost from the cycle to the atmosphere – **denitrification** – and how it can be regained from the atmosphere – **nitrogen fixation**.

Losing nitrogen from the atmosphere – denitrification

Denitrifying bacteria turn nitrate into nitrogen gas, thus losing it from the nitrogen cycle. These bacteria are anaerobes and so thrive in waterlogged soil, stagnant water and other oxygen-starved areas.

Gaining nitrogen from the atmosphere – nitrogen fixation

About 80% of the atmosphere is made up of nitrogen gas, but this is usually unavailable to living things. Molecules of N_2 gas have a triple bond ($N\equiv N$) that takes a lot of energy to break. When nitrogen gas is turned into soluble nitrogen ions, which are available to organisms, we say that nitrogen has been *fixed*. Nitrogen can be fixed during electrical storms, when the lightning provides enough energy to split the triple bond, so that the accompanying rain has dissolved nitrate in it. More reliably, however, bacteria can fix nitrogen. **Nitrogen-fixing bacteria**, mainly of the genus ***Rhizobium***, contain the enzyme **nitrogenase** that allows nitrogen gas to be fixed at low temperatures.

Nitrogen-fixing bacteria can be free-living in water or soil, but they can also occur in the roots of some plants such as **legumes** (for example, peas, beans and clover). These plants have a **mutualistic** relationship with *Rhizobium*; the plants get a supply of nitrate while the bacteria get some protection from predation and a supply of sugars. Legumes can thrive in nitrogen-poor soil. Therefore growing a legume crop and allowing it to decay in the soil is a natural way to improve soil fertility.

NB: The gene for the enzyme nitrogenase has now been isolated, which presents the possibility for it to be inserted into the genome of other plants. In theory, these too will be able to fix their own nitrogen and reduce the need for fertiliser.

The phosphorus cycle

Phosphorus is contained in several vital organic compounds, notably DNA, RNA, ATP and phospholipids. Compared to the nitrogen cycle, the **phosphorus cycle** is relatively simple because it doesn't involve the atmosphere, or the equivalent of nitrification.

1 Saprobiotic decay (by extracellular digestion – see above) releases phosphate (PO_4^-) ions into water and soil.

2 Plants and other autotrophs, such as algae, absorb the phosphate, mainly by active transport, and incorporate it into the molecules listed above.

Eutrophication

Eutrophication means 'over-fertilisation' and it is a problem that affects waterways near agricultural land. Traditionally, farmers used organic fertiliser (such as cow dung) to maintain the fertility of the soil. Today, when many farms have no animals, this is increasingly difficult and farmers turn to inorganic fertilisers that can deliver exactly the right nutrients to the crop. This can cause problems because large amounts of the fertiliser can be washed away (**leached**) into rivers and lakes. This causes a nutrient build-up that results in the water being over-fertile. This process is summarised in Fig 14.

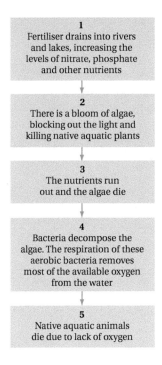

1
Fertiliser drains into rivers and lakes, increasing the levels of nitrate, phosphate and other nutrients

2
There is a bloom of algae, blocking out the light and killing native aquatic plants

3
The nutrients run out and the algae die

4
Bacteria decompose the algae. The respiration of these aerobic bacteria removes most of the available oxygen from the water

5
Native aquatic animals die due to lack of oxygen

Fig 14
A summary of eutrophication

Notes

Note that the algae themselves do not reduce the oxygen content. They photosynthesise, so actually increase the oxygen levels for a short while.

3.6 Organisms respond to changes in their internal and external environments

Animals, which by definition are multicellular, need some method of internal communication. This can be achieved either by nerves or by **hormones**.

Hormones

Hormones:

- are chemicals
- are made by endocrine glands (which have no duct (delivery tube), and secrete directly into the bloodstream)
- travel in the blood
- have an effect on particular *target cells* or *target organs*.

Many hormones are *peptides*, that is, chains of amino acids, and some are lipids, in which case they are known as *steroids*. The peptide hormones are water soluble while the steroids are lipid soluble. This is an important distinction because they work in fundamentally different ways.

In contrast, nervous communication is brought about by electrical signals called **nerve impulses**, which are transmitted down elongated specialised cells called **neurones**. The essential differences between nerves and hormones are shown in Table 5.

Table 5
The main differences between nervous and hormonal communication

Property	Nervous system	Hormonal system
Nature of signal	Impulses are ionic/electrical charge; chemical transmission at synapses	Chemical
Size of signal	Frequency modulated – determined by number of impulses sent along an axon, and the number of axons stimulated	Amplitude modulated – determined by concentration of hormone
Speed of signal	Very rapid – usually a fraction of a second	Usually slower; insulin takes minutes to act; adrenaline is very fast acting (with good reason)
Duration of signal	Very short lived	Often prolonged
Precision of signal	Very precise – for example, one part of one muscle	Often general; hormones can affect many different areas of the body at the same time
Capacity for modification	Can be modified by previous experience ('learning')	Cannot be modified by previous experience

Essential Notes

Most hormones are broken down by the liver so they do not carry on having an effect long after they have been secreted. If hormones did have a long-term effect once secretion had stopped, it would make hormonal control much less precise. Prolonged hormone action can only be achieved by prolonged secretion. A good example of this is the human growth hormone, *somatotropin*, which exerts its effect for years during childhood.

Plant hormones

There are several classes of substances that act as plant growth regulators, controlling various activities such as germination, patterns of growth, flowering, fruiting and ripening. They are often known as hormones because they are made on one part of a plant and have an effect on a different part.

3.6.1 Stimuli, both internal and external, are detected and lead to a response

3.6.1.1 Survival and response

A feature of all organisms is the ability to detect and respond to changes in their surroundings.

A **stimulus** is a change in an organism's environment (internal or external) that can be detected by **receptor** cells.

A **receptor** is a specialised cell that detects a stimulus and initiates a **nerve impulse**. Some receptors exist as individual cells (many are found in the skin, for example) while other receptors are concentrated in sense organs, such as the eye.

Taxes and **kineses** are simple behavioural responses seen in organisms that can move; for example, animals or aquatic organisms that can swim in a particular direction.

A **kinesis** is a change in the speed of random movement in response to environmental stimulus. This is seen in organisms such as woodlice. If placed in bright, dry conditions (Fig 15) they move about at random until they find somewhere that is darker and more humid, when their movements slow down and they make tighter turns. Eventually they tend to remain still when conditions are optimum.

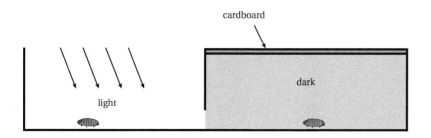

cardboard

light

dark

Fig 15
A simple **choice chamber** can be used to provide a variety of choices, most commonly light/dark and dry/humid. The woodlice cannot detect the direction of the stimuli, but they move around until, by chance, they find the conditions they prefer.

A **taxis** is a directed movement toward or away from a stimulus. There are positive and negative taxes. For example, many types of maggots can detect and move away from light, an example of a negative phototaxis. The key difference is that taxes are directional responses, while kineses are non-directional.

Tropisms are usually seen in plants, which have no muscles but can respond by growing in a particular direction (see below). Movement is slow (by human standards) and brought about by control of cell division and elongation. There are several different tropisms. Common tropisms include chemotropism (chemicals), gravitropism (gravity), hydrotropism (water), **phototropism** (lights or colours of light) and thigmotropism (touch). Movement *towards* a stimulus is a positive tropism; *away* is negative.

Auxins such as ***indole acetic acid (IAA)*** are important substances that control many different aspects of plant growth including tropisms, differentiation of tissues and abscission (leaf and fruit fall).

Auxin has a key role to play in growth following germination. Seeds are scattered in the ground and may germinate at any angle. However, the root must grow down and the shoot must grow upwards. Studies have shown that auxin is responsible for controlling this **gravitropism** (Fig 16).

Fig 16

Gravitropism
The seedling is responding to gravity: the shoot is negatively gravitropic and the root is positively gravitropic; these movements are controlled by auxin, which accumulates on the underside of the seedling.

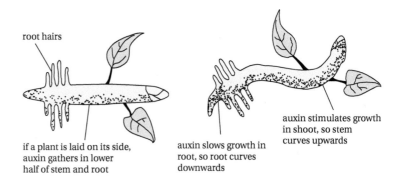

root hairs

if a plant is laid on its side, auxin gathers in lower half of stem and root

auxin slows growth in root, so root curves downwards

auxin stimulates growth in shoot, so stem curves upwards

The graph shows that at the concentrations found in the seedlings, auxin inhibits root growth and stimulates shoot growth. In the shoot, cell division and elongation along the underside are stimulated, so growth is upwards; in the root, the opposite is true.

Essential Notes

This *x*-axis is a logarithmic scale, which simply allows a large range of concentrations to fit onto one graph.

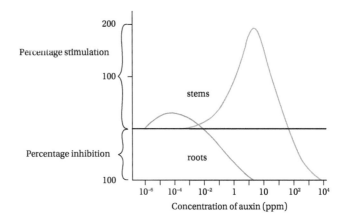

Reflex arcs

A **reflex** is a fixed movement of some part of an animal in response to a particular stimulus. Blinking and the knee jerk are familiar examples. The essential components of a reflex are:

- **Sensory neurone** – a nerve cell that carries impulses from a receptor to the central nervous system.

- **Central nervous system** (CNS) – the brain and spinal cord. The CNS processes incoming information and produces a response, often based on previous experience.

- **Motor neurone** – a nerve cell that carries impulses from the CNS to the effectors.

- **Effectors** – organs that bring about a response, usually muscles or glands.

The **reflex arc** is the simplest example of coordination, for example, blinking. In a reflex arc a particular stimulus leads to a fixed response – this is very rapid and cannot be controlled because the nerve impulses involved do not pass through the conscious parts of the brain.

Fig 17 shows an example of a reflex that avoids danger (in this case, heat) and minimises damage to the body. Other reflexes, such as the knee jerk, are postural reflexes; one of the many mechanisms we use to maintain our position and body control without having to constantly think about fine adjustments. Most reflexes are either postural or have evolved to avoid danger.

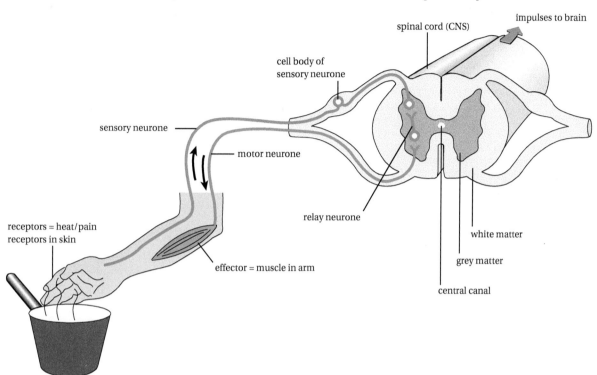

Fig 17
The reflex arc represents the most direct way of connecting a sense organ to an effector, producing the fastest possible response.

The knee jerk reaction is a three-neurone reflex arc. In this example the reflex is initiated by the stretch receptor in the patellar tendon. A tap in this tendon, just below the knee, causes the lower leg to kick forwards.

The three neurones involved are:

- A **sensory neurone** that links the receptor with the spinal cord.
- A short **relay neurone** that connects the incoming and outgoing neurones.
- The **motor neurone** that transmits impulses to the effector.

Sensory information that the knee jerk has happened also passes up the spinal cord to the brain. The response happens well before the conscious brain has a chance to stop it, but one is aware that the leg has moved.

NB: Some studies have shown that only two neurones are involved, so the sensory neurone connects directly to the motor neurone. Others show that at least one relay neurone is involved. (Do not worry too much about this.)

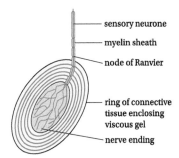

Fig 18

A cross-section through a Pacinian corpuscle. The layers of gel act as shock absorbers, preventing the receptor from being stimulated for more than a brief moment.

Essential Notes

Stretch mediated sodium channels are membrane proteins whose shape, and therefore the permeability to sodium, depend on the pressure applied to them. Increase the pressure and you change the shape, increasing the permeability.

3.6.1.2 Receptors

The Pacinian corpuscle, an example of a receptor

The **Pacinian corpuscle** is a receptor found deep in mammalian skin, where its function is to detect pressure and vibration – it is a *mechanoreceptor*. Each corpuscle consists of a single sensory neurone (often described as a 'nerve ending') surrounded by 20–60 lamellae (layers) of fibrous connective tissue separated by viscous gel (Fig 18).

A change in pressure on the corpuscle is transmitted through to the sensory nerve, which deforms, causing *stretch-mediated sodium ion channels* in the axon membrane to open. This allows sodium ions to diffuse in, creating a **generator potential**. If this potential reaches a certain level, known as a *threshold*, an impulse will pass down the sensory nerve. If the stimulus is too small, only a small amount of sodium will diffuse in, the threshold is not reached and no impulse is generated. The greater the stimulus, the higher the frequency of the impulses.

From this it can be seen that Pacinian corpuscles will detect *changes* of pressure, but not prolonged pressure. The gel acts as a 'shock absorber' – quickly redistributing to reduce the pressure on the receptor. This is called *adaptation*. No more impulses will be generated until the pressure changes again. This is an important point about receptors – they will generally respond to changes in environment, not constant stimuli.

The retina

The **retina** is a single layer of light-sensitive receptor cells – **rods** and **cones** – together with connecting neurones on the back of the eye (Figs 19a and 19b). The overall function of the retina is to gather information about the incoming light and relay it to the brain via the **optic nerve**. The actual image is formed in the brain, in the *visual cortex*.

Rods and cones differ in both their sensitivity and **visual acuity** (Table 6). Sensitivity refers to the level of light needed for the cells to function, while acuity refers to their ability to perceive detail. Rods are more sensitive than

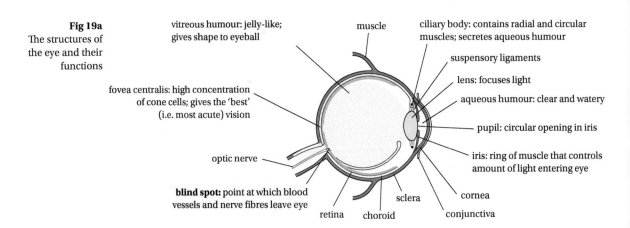

Fig 19a

The structures of the eye and their functions

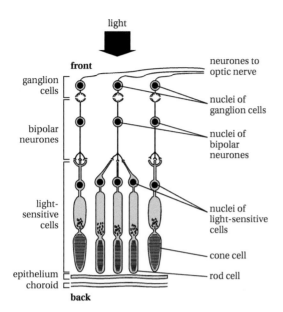

Fig 19b
The arrangement of receptor cells in the retina

Feature	Rod cells	Cone cells
Shape	Rod-shaped outer segment	Cone-shaped outer segment
Connections	Many rods converge into one neurone fovea	Only a single cone per neurone at centre of
Visual acuity	Low	High
Visual pigments	**Rhodopsin**	**Iodopsin**
Numbers	120 million per retina	Seven million per retina
Distribution	Found evenly all over retina	All over retina, but more concentrated towards fovea; the fovea itself consists only of cones
Sensitivity	Sensitive to low light intensity	Only functions in bright light
Overall function	Black-and-white vision in poor light	Seeing colour and detail in bright light

Table 6
The differences between rods and cones

cones and can function even in dim light. There are two reasons for this greater sensitivity:

1 The **rhodopsin** pigment in rod cells is more easily bleached (broken down) than the **iodopsin** pigment in the cones.

2 **Retinal convergence** – many rod cells converge into one neurone (Fig 20), so they can all contribute to the generator potential, making it more likely that the threshold will be reached; this is called *summation*.

Fig 20
The concept of retinal convergence. The cones would send impulses to the brain that would be perceived as two separate images, while the rods would show just one image.

Visual acuity

Visual acuity is the ability to distinguish objects that are close together. For instance, these lines ===== appear as two separate lines, but if you look at them from a distance they appear to blend into one thicker line. The greater the distance at which we can distinguish two lines the greater our visual acuity.

Although both rods and cones enable us to see, it is the cones that give us our high visual acuity. For example, if the letter E were to fall on the cones, we would clearly distinguish it as a letter E; if it were to fall on the rods, we would just see a blob (Fig 21).

Fig 21
Visual acuity and the fovea

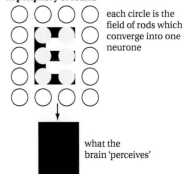

a **When an image falls on cones on fovea**

each circle is the field of cones which converge into one neurone in the optic nerve (at the centre of fovea, 1 cone = 1 neurone); the neurones coloured yellow are those which 'fire' as a result of the image

what the brain 'perceives'

b **When the same image falls on rods in periphery of retina**

each circle is the field of rods which converge into one neurone

what the brain 'perceives'

The main reason for the difference in visual acuity between the rods and cones is retinal convergence. Fig 20 shows that several rods all converge on one neurone, but each cone has its own connection. Any impulses generated by an individual cone are transmitted to the brain but any impulses generated by a rod are fed into a neurone along with impulses from many others.

The greatest concentration of cones is at a point on the retina called the **fovea**. It is only when light falls on this point that we can see things in detail (Fig 21a).

The key idea about visual acuity is that cones send more information to the brain *per unit area* of retina than is sent by the rod cells.

3.6.1.3 Control of heart rate

Each heartbeat is known as the cardiac cycle (covered in year 1, section 3.3.4.1). During the cardiac cycle, electrical impulses initiate muscular contraction, the contraction squeezes the blood, increasing the pressure and forcing blood in a particular direction.

The heart is **myogenic**, meaning that the muscle contraction originates from within the heart muscle itself. When the nerves leading to the heart are severed, it continues to beat at a slow, regular pace, but cannot be matched to the changing needs of the body. The **cardiovascular centre** in the medulla of the brain is responsible for matching heart rate to the needs of the body, but it modifies rather than initiates the beat.

The electrical impulses originate from the **sino-atrial node (SAN)** (Fig 22) and spread over the atria via specialised muscle cells, causing atrial contraction. The impulse cannot pass directly to the ventricles; there is a band of non-conducting tissue that separates the atria and the ventricles. The impulse from the SAN stimulates the **atrioventricular node** (AVN) to produce impulses that are channelled down into the ventricles by the **bundle of His**. From here impulses pass to all parts of the ventricular wall in the **Purkynje fibres**. This pathway causes a delay that gives the ventricles time to fill with blood.

> **Notes**
>
> Remember that the brain only *modifies* the rate of heartbeat.

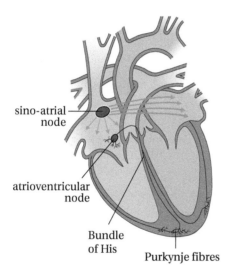

Fig 22
The conducting pathway of the heart. The arrows show the direction of the impulse that causes the cardiac muscles to contract.

sino-atrial node

atrioventricular node

Bundle of His

Purkynje fibres

The cardiovascular centre receives information from two main sources:

- The *carotid* and *aortic bodies* on the carotid artery and aorta contain **chemoreceptor** cells that are sensitive to carbon dioxide levels in the plasma. When carbon dioxide levels rise, for example, during exercise, impulses pass more frequently to the cardiovascular centre.

- Pressure receptors (**baroreceptors**) in the *carotid sinus* (a pocket in the carotid artery) transmit impulses to the cardiovascular centre when blood pressure rises. This is an essential part of the **negative feedback** system that keeps blood pressure within certain limits, thus avoiding low or high blood pressure.

> **Essential Notes**
>
> Carbon dioxide is an acidic gas. A build-up of carbon dioxide therefore lowers the pH of a solution

Essential Notes

The term antagonistic means 'opposing effects' and can apply to nerves, muscles or hormones.

There are two *antagonistic* nerves (Fig 29) leading from the cardiovascular centre to the **sino-atrial node**:

- a *sympathetic nerve*, carrying impulses that speed up the heart.
- a *parasympathetic nerve*, carrying impulses that slow down the heart.

The **sympathetic nervous system (SNS)** and the **parasympathetic nervous system (PSNS)** form part of the **autonomic nervous system (ANS)**.

When we exercise, increased carbon dioxide levels are detected and impulses are transmitted to the medulla. In response, impulses pass down the sympathetic nerve to the heart to increase the rate of the heartbeat.

Fig 29
Two nerves pass from the cardiovascular centre to the heart. If these nerves are cut, the heart continues to beat, but its rate cannot be modified.

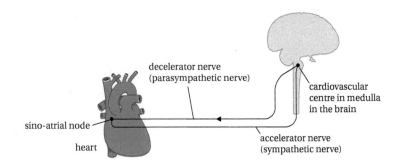

decelerator nerve (parasympathetic nerve)

cardiovascular centre in medulla in the brain

sino-atrial node

heart

accelerator nerve (sympathetic nerve)

3.6.2 Nervous coordination

3.6.2.1 Nerve impulses

A **neurone** is a nerve cell, a specialised elongated cell that is capable of carrying impulses from one end to the other. There are several types of neurones but all have the same basic features:

- a **cell body** that contains the nucleus and other organelles
- **dendrites** that take impulses towards the cell body
- an **axon** that takes impulses away from the cell body
- **synapses** that junction with other neurones or effectors (for example, muscles).

Notes

Make sure that you can distinguish between a neurone (a single nerve cell) and a nerve (a bundle of axons surrounded by connective tissue).

Fig 24 shows the basic structure of a motor neurone. Fig 25 shows how the neurone is involved in transmitting impulses. There are two processes to understand: the **resting potential**, which is basically a state of readiness, and the **action potential**, which is another name for the nerve impulse.

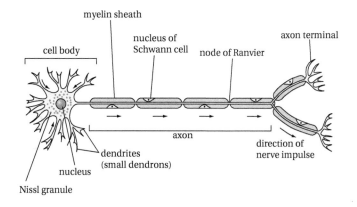

Fig 24
Basic structure of a motor neurone. All neurones have the same basic features, but the positioning of the cell body, and the number and length of the axons and dendrites, vary.

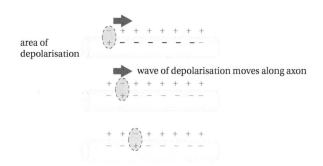

Fig 25
A nerve impulse, or action potential, is a wave of **depolarisation** that spreads along the axon; the active transport/diffusion combination quickly re-establishes the resting potential once the impulse has passed.

The resting potential

The resting potential is a 'state of readiness' and results from an unequal distribution of sodium and potassium ions, brought about by two processes: active transport and facilitated diffusion (see Fig 26).

1 **Active transport** – all animal cell membranes contain a protein pump called $Na^+K^+ATPase$. This uses the energy from splitting ATP to pump ions; three sodium ions pass out of the cell and two potassium ions move in. It is an unequal exchange; more positive ions pass out than pass in.

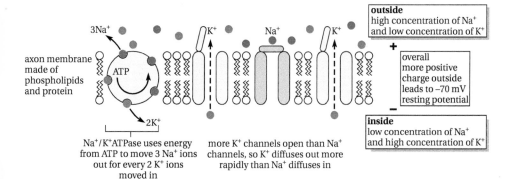

Fig 26
How a resting potential is set up across an axon membrane.

Key
● = potassium ions
● = sodium ions

Essential Notes

Normally there is a balance of positive and negative ions (notably chloride, Cl⁻). In neurones, movement of positive ions causes the resting potential.

2 **Faciliated diffusion** – there are also sodium and potassium ion channels (specific proteins) in the membrane. These channels are normally closed, but they 'leak', allowing sodium ions to diffuse in and potassium ions to leak out, down their respective concentration gradients. Generally, the potassium channels are *more leaky* than the sodium channels, so more potassium diffuses out to join the sodium ions that have been actively pumped out.

Together, these two processes cause an imbalance of Na⁺ and K⁺ ions across the membrane: there are more positive ions outside the axon. This imbalance causes a potential difference across all animal cell membranes, called the **resting potential** or the *membrane potential*. The value of this potential varies from –20 to –200 mV in different cells and species, but is usually about –70 mV.

The action potential

The **action potential** is generated when the nerve is stimulated. The stimulus might come from a receptor cell (for example, in a sense organ) or another neurone.

The action potential is brought about by a quick reversal in the permeability of the axon membrane, allowing sodium ions to flow into the axon, making the inside positive with respect to the outside (Figs 26 and 27). The sodium

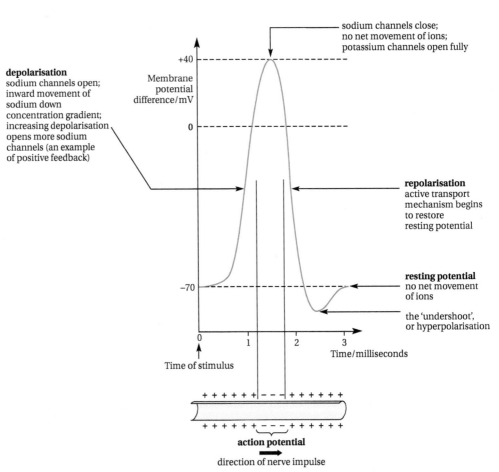

Fig 27
Electrodes placed on either side of the axon membrane produce a trace that shows the events of one impulse.

depolarisation
sodium channels open; inward movement of sodium down concentration gradient; increasing depolarisation opens more sodium channels (an example of positive feedback)

sodium channels close; no net movement of ions; potassium channels open fully

repolarisation
active transport mechanism begins to restore resting potential

resting potential
no net movement of ions

the 'undershoot', or hyperpolarisation

Membrane potential difference/mV

Time of stimulus

Time/milliseconds

action potential

direction of nerve impulse

and potassium channels are *voltage gated*, which means that they can change their shape, to let more or fewer ions pass, according to the voltage across the membrane.

The action potential has two stages: **depolarisation** and **repolarisation**.

- **Depolarisation** – step by step:

  1 When a neurone is stimulated, the voltage across the axon membrane changes.

  2 A few voltage-gated sodium channels detect this change, opening to allow some sodium to diffuse in.

  3 If the stimulus is large enough to reach the *threshold value* of about –50 mV, the rest of the voltage-gated sodium channels open for about 0.5 ms (half a millisecond, or one two-thousandths of a second).

  4 This causes sodium ions to rapidly diffuse in, making the inside of the cell more positive. This is an example of a **positive feedback** ('change creating more change') – the more Na^+ ions there are, the more the voltage changes, so the more ion channels open, and the more sodium ions diffuse in.

- **Repolarisation** – when the membrane potential reaches 0 V, the potassium channels open fully for 0.5 ms, causing potassium ions to rush out, making the inside more negative again. Since this restores the original polarity, it is called repolarisation.

Re-establishing the resting potential

The potassium channels remain fully open until after the resting potential value of –70 mV has been reached. This causes hyperpolarisation (the 'undershoot' on Fig 27) when the potential difference reaches about –80 mV. The potassium channels then close and the resting potential is established once again.

Refractory period

This is the 'recovery period' after the transmission of an action potential. There are two phases:

- **Absolute refractory period** – this is the time during which it is impossible to create another impulse, no matter how intense the stimulus.

- **Relative refractory period** – this is the time during which it is possible to create another impulse, but the stimulus needs to be greater than normal.

The refractory period is important because it keeps action potentials separate, or discrete, rather than blending together.

Action potential facts:

- An action potential is not an electrical current, nor is it a 'message'.
- All action potentials are the same size; there are no large or small impulses.
- They travel along axons at speeds up to 120 metres per second.
- The speed of transmission depends on the axon diameter (larger = faster), the number of synapses in the pathway (more = slower), temperature (higher = faster, because diffusion is faster) and whether the nerve is myelinated or not.

Saltatory conduction

Saltatory conduction occurs in myelinated nerves, when the action potential 'jumps' from node to node. This greatly increases the speed of transmission. The myelin sheath insulates the axon, and so ion exchange can only occur at the nodes of Ranvier in between the Schwann cells, where the axon membrane is exposed.

When the action potential is present at one node, the influx of Na^+ ions causes the displacement of K^+ ions down the axon (like charges repel). This diffusion of K^+ down the axon makes the next node more positive and depolarises it until the threshold is reached. In this way the impulse quickly jumps from node to node at speeds of over 100 metres per second, 10 times faster than the best sprinters. Saltatory conduction, from the Latin *saltare* meaning to jump, means jumping conduction.

As well as being faster than non-myelinated conduction, saltatory conduction is very energy efficient in terms of ATP usage. Only a small part of the axon is involved in the exchange of ions, so far fewer ions need to be pumped back after the action potential has passed.

3.6.2.2 Synaptic transmission

The synapse

Synapses are gaps between neurones. They are a vital component of the nervous system because they allow the selection of different pathways for the transmission of impulses. All our thoughts, memories, skills and actions are only possible because synapses allow us to select complex neural pathways.

The events of synaptic transmission are described as follows and in Fig 28:

1 The action potential arrives at the *synaptic knob*.

2 Calcium channels open, so Ca^{2+} ions flow into the synaptic knob.

3 The calcium ions cause vesicles containing a **transmitter substance** to move to the *presynaptic membrane*.

4 The vesicles fuse with the presynaptic membrane and discharge the transmitter into the *synaptic cleft*.

5 Molecules of transmitter diffuse across the gap and fit into specific receptor sites on the *postsynaptic membrane*.

6 The permeability of the postsynaptic membrane changes, causing a movement of ions. Na^+ ions flow inwards, building up a charge known as **EPSP** (excitatory postsynaptic potential).

7 If the EPSP reaches a threshold, an action potential is generated in the neurone.

8 The transmitter substance is broken down by an enzyme in the cleft.

9 The products of breakdown are reabsorbed into the synaptic knob, where they are re-synthesised using energy from ATP synthesised by the mitochondria.

Notes

Always refer to action potentials as impulses, not messages. Messages are complex, whereas nerve impulses are simply electrical 'blips'.

Impulses do not cross synapses. An impulse comes to an end once it reaches a synapse. After synaptic transmission, a new impulse is generated.

Essential Notes

Calcium ions are actively pumped out of the synaptic knob between impulses so that there is a diffusion gradient. When an impulse arrives, calcium channels open so calcium diffuses in; after that, it is pumped out again.

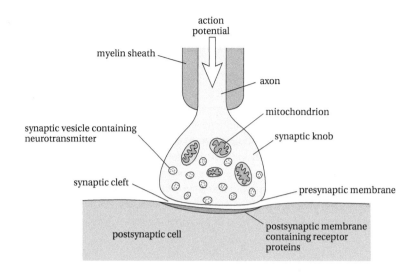

Fig 28a
The basic structure of the synapse

Fig 28b
The sequence of events (1-9) in chemical transmission at a synapse

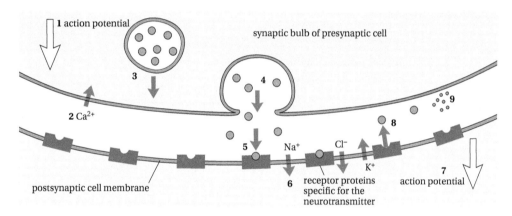

NB: All the events in synaptic transmission take place in about one hundredth of a second. Transmission across synapses is *unidirectional* (in one direction only), because the transmitter is made only on the presynaptic side and the receptor proteins are found only on the postsynaptic side. This prevents impulses being transmitted in the wrong direction.

The most widespread transmitter is **acetylcholine (Ach)**, which is found in the synapses of most voluntary nerves, including **neuromuscular junctions**. The sympathetic nervous system (SNS) uses *noradrenaline*, while the brain has many different transmitters, including *serotonin* and *dopamine*.

Synapses that release acetylcholine are said to be **cholinergic synapses**. In these synapses the enzyme **acetylcholinesterase** is found in the cleft, where it breaks down the transmitter once the impulse has been generated. This prevents prolonged stimulation. Acetylcholine is broken down into choline and acetic acid, which are re-absorbed into the presynaptic membrane where they are re-combined into active transmitter.

Notes

Many drugs and toxins work by affecting synaptic transmission in some way. You are not expected to learn the mode of action of a wide variety of drugs and toxins. Exam questions will test your understanding of synaptic transmission (outlined on the previous pages) by using the example of a particular drug or toxin.

Inhibition at synapses

If every nerve impulse that arrived at a synapse succeeded in setting up impulses in the next neurone, the result would be chaos. The significance of synapses is that they allow us to select particular pathways. Thus, at any one time many more synapses need inhibiting than need stimulating. For this reason there are inhibitory neurones. Impulses arriving at synapses of inhibitory neurones make it more difficult for an action potential to be generated. The neurotransmitters from these synapses open potassium and chloride channels rather than sodium channels, and the resulting ion movement causes an **IPSP** (inhibitory postsynaptic potential) in which the postsynaptic membranes are hyperpolarised (to about –90 mV) rather than depolarised. The balance of inhibition and stimulation received at a particular synapse will determine whether an action potential is generated or not.

Temporal and spatial summation

Summation means 'to add up' and refers to the fact that any particular action potential arriving at a synapse might not be enough to generate an action potential in the postsynaptic neurone, but two or more might. There are two types of summation:

- **Temporal summation** ('in time') – where two or more impulses arrive in quick succession *down the same neurone.*

- **Spatial summation** ('in space') – where two or more impulses arrive at the *same time down different neurones.*

In both cases, summation is achieved because each impulse causes more transmitter to be released, contributing to the EPSP and making it more likely that the threshold will be reached.

3.6.3 Skeletal muscles are stimulated to contract by nerves and act as effectors

Muscle is a remarkable tissue that has the ability to contract. Broadly speaking there are three types of muscle in the body: smooth, cardiac and skeletal, as follows:

1 **Smooth muscle** – is generally found in tubular organs such as the intestines, blood vessels and reproductive system where its function is peristalsis.

2 **Cardiac muscle** – is only found in the heart.

3 **Skeletal muscle** – is attached to bones where its function is to produce movement and maintain posture. Contraction of skeletal muscle is the key topic you need to learn.

Muscles work in antagonistic pairs

Muscle is a tissue with just one ability; it can contract. It can only produce movement when it pulls on an incompressible skeleton, i.e. hard bone. Muscles can pull but not push, so they work in **antagonistic** pairs or groups. For example, the biceps and the triceps muscles in the upper arm act antagonistically to bend ('flex') or straighten ('extend') the arm. When a muscle contracts, it pulls on a tendon which in turn pulls on the bone. Importantly, not all contractions produce movement; many muscles stabilise the body, allowing maintenance of posture.

Essential Notes

The word *antagonistic* means opposing. There are antagonistic muscles, nerves and hormones.

Skeletal muscle

Fig 29 shows the basic structure of skeletal muscle. The key unit is the **sarcomere** – one short length of a muscle fibre in which the pattern of bands is repeated. The changes in this banding pattern when muscle contracts reveal a lot about muscular contraction, making it a favourite topic for exam questions.

Some skeletal muscle facts:

- An individual muscle is made up of hundreds of cylindrical *muscle fibres*, about 50 μm in diameter and ranging in length from a few millimetres to several centimetres.
- Muscle fibres are not composed of individual cells – the cell membranes have broken down and so each fibre has many nuclei.
- Each fibre is surrounded by a modified cell membrane called the *sarcolemma*.
- Each muscle fibre is composed of many long, cylindrical **myofibrils**, consisting of a repeating arrangement of proteins, which causes the banding pattern.
- Each repeated pattern of proteins is called a sarcomere.
- The two main proteins involved in muscular contraction are **actin** (thin) and **myosin** (thick) filaments.
- Muscles contract when the actin fibres are pulled over the myosin fibres.
- Two other proteins involved are **tropomyosin**, and **troponin**.

Tropomyosin winds around the actin filament, preventing it from binding to myosin. Troponin, a globular protein, moves the tropomyosin out of the way. This allows actin to bind to myosin, thus initiating muscular contraction.

Within each sarcomere there are two light bands: the I zone consisting of only actin filaments, and the H zone that consists of only myosin. Between them are darker areas where these proteins overlap. When muscles contract, the actin and myosin filaments are pulled over each other so that the light bands get smaller. Note that the width of the dark band corresponds to the width of the myosin molecules, so it does not get any narrower – molecules do not shrink, they just slide over each other.

The sliding filament theory of muscle contraction

The basic steps in muscular contraction:

1　An impulse arrives down a motor nerve and terminates at the **neuromuscular junction** (a modified synapse).

2　The synapse secretes acetylcholine.

3　Acetylcholine fits into receptor sites on the *motor end plate*.

4　The binding causes a change in the permeability of the **sarcoplasmic reticulum**, resulting in an influx of calcium ions into the *myofilament*.

5　The calcium ions bind to the troponin, changing its shape.

6　Troponin displaces the tropomyosin, so that the myosin heads can bind to the actin.

Essential Notes

Sarcoplasmic reticulum is modified endoplasmic reticulum - a network of membranes that surround the myofilaments.

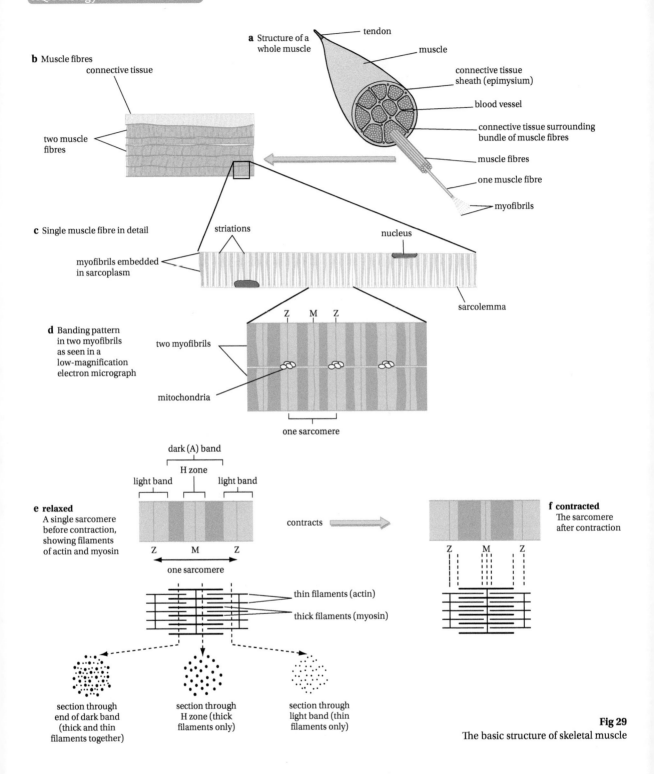

a Structure of a whole muscle
tendon
muscle
connective tissue sheath (epimysium)
blood vessel
connective tissue surrounding bundle of muscle fibres
muscle fibres
one muscle fibre
myofibrils

b Muscle fibres
connective tissue
two muscle fibres

c Single muscle fibre in detail
striations
nucleus
myofibrils embedded in sarcoplasm
sarcolemma

d Banding pattern in two myofibrils as seen in a low-magnification electron micrograph
Z M Z
two myofibrils
mitochondria
one sarcomere

dark (A) band
H zone
light band
light band

e relaxed
A single sarcomere before contraction, showing filaments of actin and myosin
Z M Z
one sarcomere

contracts

f contracted
The sarcomere after contraction
Z M Z

thin filaments (actin)
thick filaments (myosin)

section through end of dark band (thick and thin filaments together)
section through H zone (thick filaments only)
section through light band (thin filaments only)

Fig 29
The basic structure of skeletal muscle

7   The myosin head pulls backwards, so that the actin is pulled over the myosin. This is the 'power stroke'.

8   An ATP molecule becomes fixed to the myosin head, causing it to detach from the actin.

9   The splitting of ATP provides the energy to move the myosin head back to its original position, 'cocking the trigger' again.

10   The myosin head again becomes attached to the actin, but further along.

11   In this way, the actin is quickly pulled over the myosin in a ratchet motion, shortening the sarcomere, the whole filament and the muscle.

The role of ATP and phosphocreatine

The energy for muscular contraction comes from ATP, but during intense exercise the ATP runs out after about three seconds. After this, ATP is quickly re-synthesised using phosphate derived from the splitting of **phosphocreatine (PC)**. The ATP/PC system can provide enough energy for maximum effort – a sprint, for example – for up to 10 seconds. After this, for up to about one minute, ATP is supplied from glycolysis, the first stage of respiration. This second system can still provide enough energy for maximum effort, but it is anaerobic, and lactate build up is a painful problem.

After about a minute, supplies of ATP come from full aerobic respiration. The disadvantage of aerobic respiration is that it can only provide ATP quickly enough for exercise at about 60%–70% of maximum capacity, but the good news is that this system can keep going as long as there is fuel (glucose or lipid) and there is no build up of lactate.

Slow- and fast-twitch muscle fibres

There are two different types of skeletal muscle fibres:

- **Fast-twitch fibres** contract quickly and powerfully, but fatigue quickly. They rely on glycolysis for their ATP, and so lactate builds up rapidly. Athletes who specialise in power events such as short sprints, throwing, jumping and weightlifting tend to have more fast-twitch fibres.

- **Slow-twitch fibres** contract more slowly, producing less power, but they have the advantage of not tiring so quickly and so they can keep going for long periods. Slow-twitch fibres rely on aerobic respiration for their ATP, and have more mitochondria than fast-twitch fibres.

Individuals are born with a certain balance of fast- and slow-twitch fibres. It is thought that training can alter the balance but there is no conclusive proof of this.

Essential Notes

Phosphocreatine is also called creatine phosphate, so in this context PC and CP can refer to the same substance.

3.6.4 Homeostasis is the maintenance of a stable internal environment

3.6.4.1 Principles of homeostasis and negative feedback

Homeostasis is the ability of an organism to maintain its internal conditions within certain limits. In humans, examples of homeostasis include:

- maintaining the pH of blood and body fluids between 7.3 and 7.45
- maintaining the core body temperature at around 37 °C
- maintaining blood glucose levels between 4 and 11 millimoles per litre.

You can see from these examples that internal conditions are not absolutely constant, but are maintained within fairly narrow limits.

There are many other examples of homeostasis, such as the maintenance of all the different hormone levels and the many components of blood plasma. You need to know about the control of blood glucose levels and blood water potential.

Negative feedback – the mechanism of homeostasis

Most examples of homeostasis involve **negative feedback**. When a factor changes, the homeostatic mechanism acts to reverse that change and bring things back to normal. Fig 30 shows a negative feedback loop and how it differs from **positive feedback**.

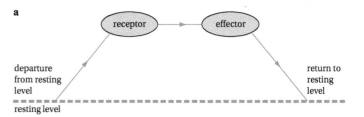

Notes

When you discuss an example of homeostasis – in longer exam questions, for example – it is important to consider all of the following:

1 What causes the level to change?

2 What detects the change?

3 How is the change reversed?

Fig 30
A negative feedback loop and how it differs from positive feedback

a Negative feedback is a mechanism that keeps levels constant
b In contrast, positive feedback is a mechanism for bringing about change

3.6.4.2 Control of blood glucose concentration

Regulation of blood glucose levels

Blood glucose levels need to be kept within certain limits. Glucose is the body's main respiratory fuel, so while a plentiful supply should be in circulation, too much glucose lowers the water potential of the blood.

Too much blood glucose – *hyperglycaemia* – will lower the **water potential** of the blood and produce symptoms of thirst and (as a result of fluid intake) frequent urination. In contrast, too little glucose, *hypoglycaemia* – will produce symptoms of dizziness, tiredness, lack of concentration, irritability and, in extreme cases, coma and death. This is because the brain must have glucose, it cannot use alternative fuels such as lipids.

The *pancreas* is the key organ in the control of blood glucose levels because it makes the hormones **insulin** and **glucagon**. Over 90% of the pancreas is dedicated to making pancreatic juice, but there are small patches of cells, the **islets of Langerhans**, that make and secrete hormones (see Fig 31). The islets consist of two types of cells; α (alpha) cells and β (beta) cells. The β cells secrete insulin and the α cells secrete glucagon. These hormones are *antagonistic*; they have opposing effects.

Essential Notes

Insulin is a relatively small protein, consisting of 51 amino acids in two polypeptide chains.

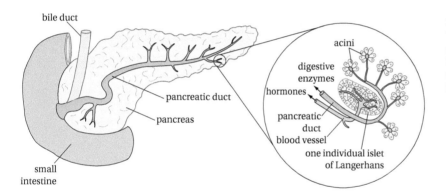

Fig 31
The major part of the pancreas makes a juice containing digestive enzymes, but small patches of endocrine cells, the islets of Langerhans, produce the hormones insulin and glucagon.

> **Definition**
>
> *These definitions are useful for this topic:*
>
> **Glycogenesis** – *the production of **glycogen** by the polymerisation of glucose.*
>
> **Glycogenolysis** – *the breakdown of glycogen to release glucose.*
>
> **Gluconeogenesis** – *the production of glucose from non-carbohydrate sources (i.e. lipid or protein, but not glycogen). This happens during fasting/dieting/starvation, when glucose and glycogen levels are low.*

Notes

The terms glycogenesis, glycogenolysis and gluconeogenesis look similar and it is easy to confuse them. Look at the key parts of the words: *genesis* = creation, *lysis* = splitting, *neo* = new.

Essential Notes

The control of blood glucose is unusual because the receptors and the effectors are the same cells. With most homeostatic mechanisms, the receptors and the effectors are separate cells/organs, and have to communicate via nerves or hormones.

If blood sugar levels are too high ...

Blood glucose levels usually rise for a few hours after a meal, as the sugars and starches are digested into glucose and absorbed into the blood. When the β (beta) cells in the islets of Langerhans detect a rise in blood glucose, they respond by secreting the hormone insulin. Insulin travels to all parts of the body but the target cells containing insulin receptors are mainly those of the liver, muscles and adipose (fat storage) tissue.

When insulin binds with insulin receptors, it sets in motion a series of events that results in vesicles containing glucose channel proteins moving to the cell surface membrane. When these proteins join the membrane, the facilitated diffusion of glucose increases (Fig 32), glucose passes from the blood into the cells and so blood glucose levels fall.

Fig 32
Insulin binds to specific insulin receptor proteins in cell membranes, activating a mechanism that opens extra glucose channels. In this way glucose molecules pass out of the blood and into cells. This process, by definition, is facilitated diffusion.

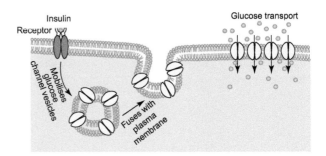

Insulin also activates enzyme pathways that convert glucose into **glycogen**, protein or lipid (**glycogenesis**).

Type 1 diabetes

Insulin-dependent diabetics, known as type 1 diabetics, cannot make insulin and so glucose cannot pass from blood into cells when needed. Blood glucose levels can then rise – causing hyperglycaemia – while the cells are starved of fuel. Symptoms include:

- **Thirst** – the high glucose levels decrease the water potential of the blood, stimulating the sensation of thirst.

- **Glucose in the urine** – the kidneys normally reabsorb all glucose, but when blood glucose levels are high they are unable to do so.

- **Weight loss** – when starved of their main fuel, cells respire other fuels such as lipids.

- **Breath smells of ketones** (a fruity smell) – ketones are a by-product of lipid metabolism.

- **Excessive urination** – a consequence of the increased fluid intake.

Only about 10%–15% of all diabetics have type 1 diabetes, and it tends to develop in people under the age of 40, often in young children. It is an auto-immune disease in which the body's own immune system destroys the insulin-producing cells. Treatment involves monitoring blood glucose levels, and injections of carefully judged amounts of slow-acting and fast-acting insulin. Each individual learns to manage his or her own condition, recognising early warning symptoms of hyper- or hypoglycaemia, and balancing the diet and exercise with insulin injections.

Type 2 diabetes

This is known as late onset diabetes and is becoming increasingly common due to the high rate of obesity. It is also becoming more common in younger people. Of all diabetics, 85%–90% have type 2 diabetes. The problem is that either the body does not make enough insulin, or that the cells do not respond to it properly. Treatment usually involves a combination of diet, exercise and weight loss.

If blood glucose levels are too low ...

When the α (alpha) cells in the islets of Langerhans detect a fall in blood glucose, they respond by secreting the hormone glucagon. The target cells for glucagon are largely the same as those for insulin.

When glucagon binds to its receptor, it sets in motion a cascade of reactions. Firstly, the enzyme **adenyl cyclase** is activated, which in turn converts ATP into **cyclic AMP**, which is the 'second messenger' in the cell (Fig 33). Cyclic AMP brings about the activation of the enzymes that convert glycogen into glucose.

Essential Notes

Insulin and glucagon are water-soluble. These hormones do not enter their target cells. Instead, they exert their effect via a second messenger (cyclic AMP) in the cell. In contrast, steroid hormones (such as oestrogen) are lipid-soluble and pass straight into the cell.

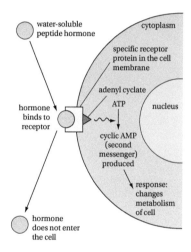

Fig 33
Water-soluble hormones work via a second messenger which is formed inside the cell when the hormone binds to its membrane receptor.

3.6.4.3 Control of blood water potential

It is a vital aspect of homeostasis to control the **water potential** of the blood and body fluids, otherwise cells either shrink or swell as they lose or gain water by osmosis. The control of water potential is known as **osmoregulation**, and the key organs are the kidneys, which operate via two basic processes:

1 **Ultrafiltration** (filtration under pressure). This produces **filtrate**, which is basically the same composition as tissue fluid.

2 **Selective reabsorption and secretion.** The nephron will reabsorb some substances back into the blood, but not others. Generally it will reabsorb all the glucose and amino acids, and will reabsorb a varying amount of water depending on the body's state of dehydration.

The structure of the kidney

Each kidney consists of about a thousand **nephrons**, tightly packed together and surrounded by a dense network of blood vessels (Fig 34). The urine made by the kidneys drains into the **ureters**, which take the fluid to the bladder.

Essential Notes

You may remember from year 1, topic 3, that tissue fluid is basically blood plasma without the proteins that are too large to pass across the capillary wall

The nephron

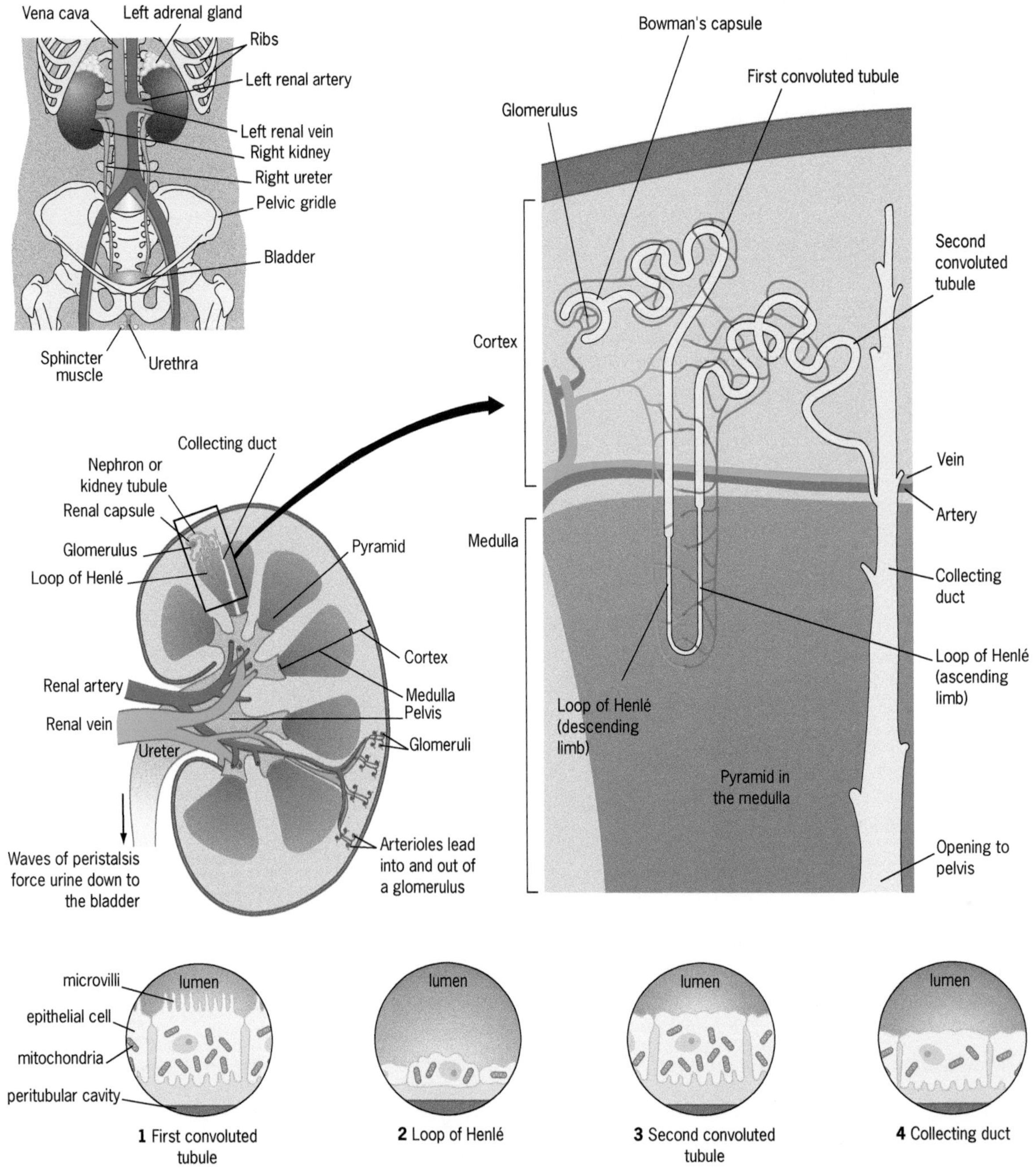

Vena cava
Left adrenal gland
Ribs
Left renal artery
Left renal vein
Right kidney
Right ureter
Pelvic gridle
Bladder
Sphincter muscle
Urethra

Collecting duct
Nephron or kidney tubule
Renal capsule
Glomerulus
Loop of Henlé
Renal artery
Renal vein
Ureter
Waves of peristalsis force urine down to the bladder
Pyramid
Cortex
Medulla
Pelvis
Glomeruli
Arterioles lead into and out of a glomerulus

Bowman's capsule
First convoluted tubule
Glomerulus
Cortex
Medulla
Second convoluted tubule
Vein
Artery
Collecting duct
Loop of Henlé (ascending limb)
Loop of Henlé (descending limb)
Pyramid in the medulla
Opening to pelvis

microvilli
epithelial cell
mitochondria
peritubular cavity
lumen

1 First convoluted tubule
2 Loop of Henlé
3 Second convoluted tubule
4 Collecting duct

Fig 34
Gross structure of the kidney. The cortex (outer part) of the kidney consists of the Bowman's capsules and the tubules (PCT, proximal convoluted tubule; and DCT, distal convoluted tubule), while the medulla (central part) consists of the loops of Henlé and collecting ducts.

As shown in Fig 34, each nephron consists of five main regions:

1 **Bowman's capsule.** This is the top end of the nephron, and is shaped like a wine glass. It contains a knot of blood vessels called the **glomerulus**. This is the region where the blood is filtered to produce filtrate.

2 The **proximal (or first) convoluted tubule** (PCT). Most of the filtrate is immediately reabsorbed into the blood.

3 The **loop of Henlé** – a hairpin-shaped loop that is the key to water conservation in dry conditions.

4 The **distal (or second) convoluted tubule** where a lot of the 'fine tuning' of the filtrate takes place. Substances are reabsorbed or excreted according to the needs of the body.

5 The **collecting duct** – the final part of the nephron is where a lot of water is reabsorbed. The fluid that passes out of the collecting duct is urine.

It is important to appreciate that the blood vessels that come out of the glomerulus wrap around the rest of nephron. It is this close association between the nephron and the blood that allows the exchange of substances that ultimately leads to urine formation.

The formation of glomerular filtrate in Bowman's capsule

The function of the Bowman's capsule is to make the filtrate, which it does by **ultrafiltration** – filtration under pressure. The entrance to the glomerulus is wider than the exit, with the result that the hydrostatic pressure is increased and blood is forced against a three-layer filter. This physical filter effectively removes the barrier of the selectively permeable cell-surface membrane, and filters according to size. The critical layer is the basement layer, the mesh of which is too small to allow proteins and cells through.

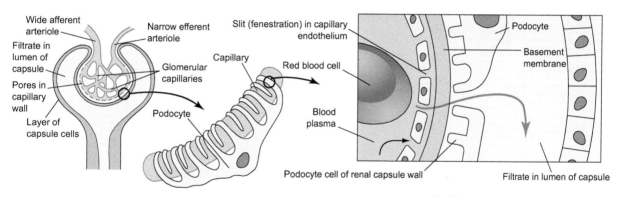

Fig 35
The fine structure of the Bowman's capsule

The three layers of the filter are (Fig 35):

1 The **endothelium** of the capillary. The cells have gaps in between them called fenestrations that help the filtration process.

2 The cells lining the tubule. These are called **podocytes** because they appear to have feet.

3 A **basement membrane**. This is a continuous sheet of protein between the other two layers of cells. It forms a continuous mesh and as such is the finest part of the filter, preventing the larger protein molecules from leaving the blood.

The filtrate that results has the same composition as tissue fluid: blood plasma without the large proteins. If we simply excreted this filtrate we would become dehydrated very quickly, and would lose large amounts of vital nutrients such as glucose and amino acids. What needs to happen now is that most of the filtrate is reabsorbed, so that we only excrete what we don't need.

Reabsorption by the proximal convoluted tubule

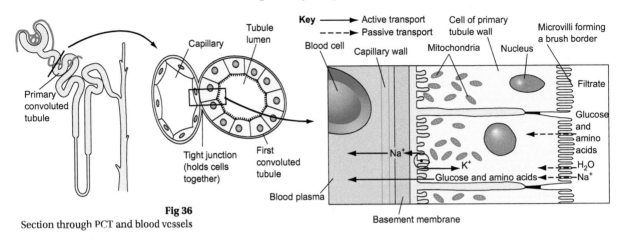

Fig 36
Section through PCT and blood vessels

The proximal convoluted tubule (PCT) is the main region of reabsorption, which occurs by a combination of facilitated diffusion and active transport. Glucose, amino acids and most ions are reabsorbed into the blood and, as a consequence, water follows these solutes by osmosis. For every 100 cm^3 of filtrate formed, about 99 cm^3 passes straight back into the blood. The nephron performs its homeostatic function by adding to or reabsorbing from the fluid that is left. In this way, filtrate is turned into urine.

Fig 37
How the loop of Henlé works.
The numbers refer to the solute concentration in mg per 100 cm^3.

The role of the loop of Henlé

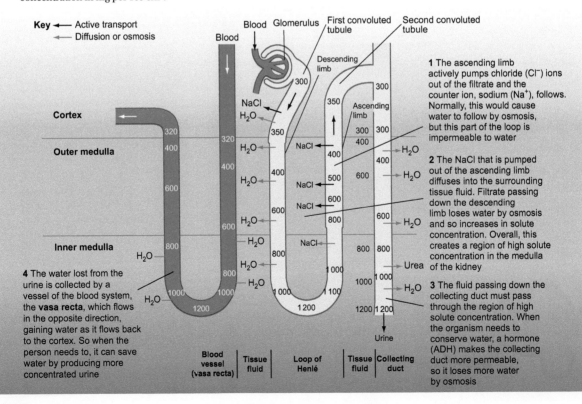

1 The ascending limb actively pumps chloride (Cl$^-$) ions out of the filtrate and the counter ion, sodium (Na$^+$), follows. Normally, this would cause water to follow by osmosis, but this part of the loop is impermeable to water

2 The NaCl that is pumped out of the ascending limb diffuses into the surrounding tissue fluid. Filtrate passing down the descending limb loses water by osmosis and so increases in solute concentration. Overall, this creates a region of high solute concentration in the medulla of the kidney

3 The fluid passing down the collecting duct must pass through the region of high solute concentration. When the organism needs to conserve water, a hormone (ADH) makes the collecting duct more permeable, so it loses more water by osmosis

4 The water lost from the urine is collected by a vessel of the blood system, the **vasa recta**, which flows in the opposite direction, gaining water as it flows back to the cortex. So when the person needs to, it can save water by producing more concentrated urine

The loop of Henlé consists of a **descending limb**, which takes filtrate down into the medulla, and an **ascending limb**, which brings it back to the cortex. Surrounding the loop is a network of blood capillaries known as the **vasa recta**.

How the loop of Henlé works (Fig 37):

Step 1 As filtrate passes down the descending limb, water leaves by osmosis due to the higher salt concentration in the surrounding fluid (see step 2). Water passes through channel proteins in the cell membrane called **aquaporins**. The longer the loop, the more water flows out of the filtrate and the lower the water potential of the filtrate.

Step 2 As filtrate flows up the ascending limb, sodium, potassium and chloride ions are pumped out of the filtrate by active transport, resulting in the high concentration of salt in the surrounding fluid. The ascending limb is impermeable to water, so water cannot follow the solute by osmosis.

Overall, the loop creates a region of high salt concentration (a 'sodium gradient'), and very low water potential, through which the collecting duct must pass.

Dependent on how permeable the collecting duct is to water – a factor that is largely under hormonal control (see below) – the salt will draw water out of the collecting duct by osmosis so that it is conserved in the body.

The distal convoluted tubule (DCT)

The permeability of the DCT to water is, to some extent, under the influence of ADH – see below – though the role of the loop of Henlé and the collecting duct are more significant in controlling water potential.

The control of water potential

A **negative feedback** system operates to control the water potential of the blood. If water loss exceeds water intake, the fall in the blood's water potential is detected by **osmoreceptor cells** in the **hypothalamus**. In response, the hypothalamus stimulates the posterior (rear) lobe of the **pituitary gland** to release **antidiuretic hormone (ADH)**. Diuresis is the production of urine, so this hormone slows down that process.

ADH is a peptide hormone (a short chain of amino acids) whose target organ is the collecting duct (and to some extent the DCT) of the nephron. ADH makes the collecting duct more permeable to water, by acting on proteins called **aquaporins**. In a similar way to insulin activating more glucose transport proteins, ADH stimulates more aquaporins to join the membrane of the collecting duct cells, making it more permeable to water.

When the walls of the duct are permeable to water, the low water potential of the surrounding fluid – the region of high salt concentration created by the loop of Henlé – draws water out by osmosis. This results in more water leaving the duct and re-entering the blood. In this way water is conserved, and the urine has a lower water potential, which is why it becomes dark. So ADH acts to return the water potential of the blood to within normal limits. As with all negative feedbacks, the receptor cells in the hypothalamus monitor the change and switch off this corrective mechanism when the water potential of the blood returns to an acceptable level.

Essential Notes

Animals that live in arid (dry) environments often have an extra-long loop of Henlé, which allows them to make urine with a very low water potential.

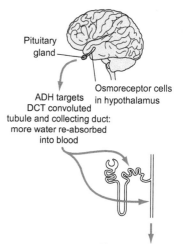

Pituitary gland

Osmoreceptor cells in hypothalamus

ADH targets DCT convoluted tubule and collecting duct: more water re-absorbed into blood

More concentrated urine

Fig 38 The hypothalamus and the pituitary

Practical and mathematical skills

In both the AS and A level papers at least 15% of marks will be allocated to the assessment of skills related to practical work. A minimum of 10% of the marks will be allocated to assessing mathematical skills at level 2 and above. These practical and mathematical skills are likely to overlap to some extent; for example, applying mathematical concepts to analysing given data and in plotting and interpretation of graphs.

The required practical activities assessed at AS are:

● Investigation into the effect of a named variable on the rate of an enzyme-controlled reaction

● Preparation of stained squashes of cells from plant root tips; setup and use of an optical microscope to identify the stages of mitosis in these stained squashes and calculation of a mitotic index

● Production of a dilution series of a solute to produce a calibration curve with which to identify the water potential of plant tissue

● Investigation into the effect of a named variable on the permeability of cell-surface membranes

● Dissection of animal or plant gas exchange system or mass transport system or of organ within such a system

● Use of aseptic techniques to investigate the effect of antimicrobial substances on microbial growth.

The additional required practical activities assessed only at A level are:

● Use of chromatography to investigate the pigments isolated from leaves of different plants, e.g. leaves from shade-tolerant and shade-intolerant plants or leaves of different colours

● Investigation into the effect of a named factor on the rate of dehydrogenase activity in extracts of chloroplasts

● Investigation into the effect of a named variable on the rate of respiration of cultures of single-celled organisms

● Investigation into the effect of an environmental variable on the movement of an animal using either a choice chamber or a maze

● Production of a dilution series of a glucose solution and use of colorimetric techniques to produce a calibration curve with which to identify the concentration of glucose in an unknown 'urine' sample

● Investigation into the effect of a named environmental factor on the distribution of a given species.

Questions will assess the ability to understand in detail how to ensure that the use of instruments, equipment and techniques leads to results that are as accurate as possible. The list of apparatus and techniques is given in the specification.

Exam questions may require problem solving and application of scientific knowledge in practical contexts, including novel contexts.

Exam questions may also ask for critical comments on a given experimental method, conclusions from given observations or require the presentation of data in appropriate ways such as in tables or graphs. It will also be necessary to express numerical results to an appropriate precision with reference to uncertainties and errors; for example, in thermometer readings.

The mathematical skills assessed are given in the specification.

Practice exam-style questions

1 A group of students were given some maggots that are always found in dark environments. They were given two alternative explanations.

Alternative 1: The maggots are moving directly from the direction of the light source in a straight line towards the dark.

Alternative 2: They are crawling around in random directions, making turns until they happen to reach the preferred half, where they remain.

(a) What type of response is being described in each of these alternatives?

Alternative 1 _____

Alternative 2 _____ 2 marks

(b) Suggest how you would set about finding out which alternative is the more likely explanation.

_____

_____

_____

_____ 4 marks

Total marks: 6

2 The woodmouse *Apodemus sylvaticus* (also called the long-tailed field mouse), is part of the woodland food chain shown below (Fig E1).

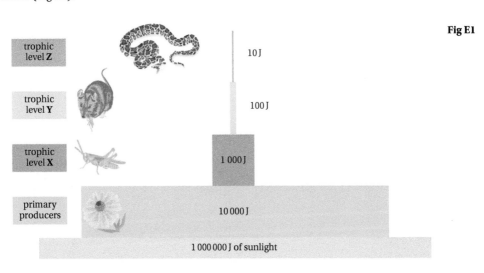

Fig E1

(a) Name trophic level X.

_____ 1 mark

(b) Explain why so little of the energy in the producers is transferred to trophic level Y.

_____

_____

_____ 3 marks

Total marks: 4

3 The diagram below (Fig E2) illustrates the energy conversion efficiency of one particular species of caterpillar.

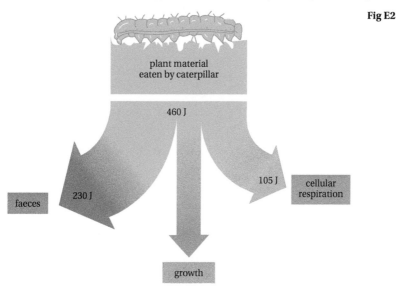

Fig E2

(a) **(i)** Calculate the amount of energy that is incorporated into the tissues of the caterpillar.

Answer = _____ J   1 mark

(ii) Calculate the percentage efficiency of the energy conversion at this trophic level.

_____

_____ 2 marks

(b) Explain why such a lot of energy is lost in the faeces.

_____

_____ 2 marks

(c) Suggest how the pattern of energy loss would be different if this herbivore was a mammal such as a rabbit. Explain your answer.

_____

_____ 2 marks

(d) Explain how the carbon contained in the faeces could be used by a plant to make sugars.

_____

_____

_____

_____ 4 marks

Total marks: 11

4 The graph (Fig E3) shows the distribution of rods and cones in the human retina.

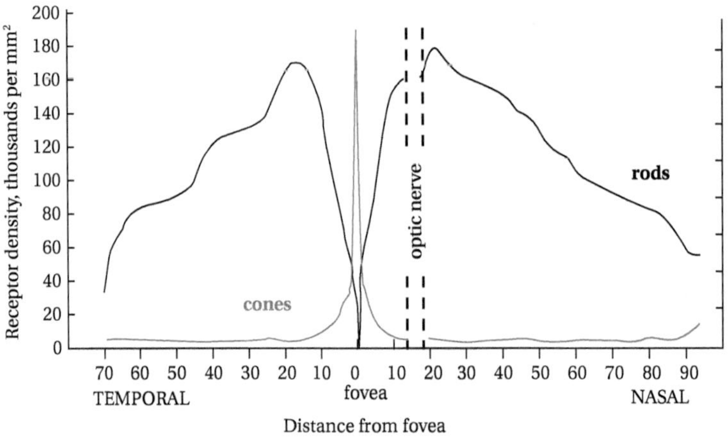

Fig E3

(a) Describe the distribution of rods and cones across the retina.

_____

_____

_____ 3 marks

(b) What is the total receptor density at 50 units from the fovea on the temporal side?

_____ 1 mark

(c) Use the graph to explain why we can still distinguish the colour of an object when viewed out of the corner of the eye.

_____ 1 mark

(d) There is little difference in the peak density of rods and cones. Explain why visual acuity is much greater with the cones.

_____

_____ 2 marks

Total marks: 7

5 The diagram (Fig E4) shows a reflex arc.

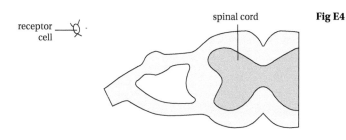

Fig E4

spinal cord

receptor cell

effector (muscle)

(a) Complete the diagram of a reflex arc by drawing and labelling the sensory neurone, relay neurone and motor neurone.

_____

_____

_____ 3 marks

(b) List three features of reflex arcs.

_____

_____

_____ 3 marks

(c) Explain how the structure of a synapse prevents impulses being passed in both directions.

_____

_____ 2 marks

Total marks: 8

6 A single Pacinian corpuscle (pressure receptor) in the skin was isolated and stimulated with a period of light pressure followed by a period of heavier pressure (Fig E5). The trace shows the action potentials that passed down the sensory neurone.

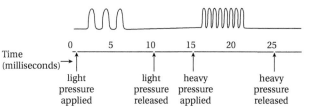

Fig E5

Time (milliseconds)

0   5   10   15   20   25

light pressure applied

light pressure released

heavy pressure applied

heavy pressure released

(a) Explain how the trace illustrates the '**all or nothing**' principle.

_____

_____ 2 marks

(b) Use the diagram to explain how the body distinguishes between stimuli of different intensities.

_____ 1 mark

(c) **(i)** Explain why the impulses stop before the stimulus ends.

_____

_____ 2 marks

(ii) Suggest the advantage of this property.

_____

_____ 2 marks

Total marks: 7

7 Steps (i) to (viii) are events that occur in synaptic transmission.

(i) Calcium ions activate vesicles.

(ii) Transmitter diffuses across synaptic cleft.

(iii) EPSP builds up.

(iv) Calcium ions diffuse into synaptic knob.

(v) Threshold is reached.

(vi) Action potential arrives at synaptic knob.

(vii) Sodium ions diffuse into postsynaptic cleft.

(viii) Transmitter fits into receptors on postsynaptic membrane.

(a) List the events in the correct order.

_____

_____ 2 marks

(b) Explain why the presence of mitochondria is essential at the synaptic knob.

_____

_____

_____ 3 marks

The krait is a venomous snake whose bite contains a powerful neurotoxin called bungarotoxin. The toxin blocks the acetylcholine receptor sites on neuromuscular junctions.

(c) Explain what effect bungarotoxin will have on anyone who is bitten.

_____

_____ 2 marks

Total marks: 7

8   The diagram (Fig E6) shows the banding pattern in one sarcomere of skeletal muscle.

Relaxed sarcomere   **Fig E6**

Z   M   Z

dark
band

(a) Draw or describe the sarcomere as it would appear when contracted.

_____

_____ 2 marks

(b) Outline the role of calcium ions in muscular contraction.

_____

_____

_____ 3 marks

The muscle fibre types of a selection of age-matched athletes were analysed, and the results are summarised in the table below. These are average values; there is considerable variation between athletes.

Type of athlete	Approx. % fast-twitch	Approx. % slow-twitch
Marathon runner	18	82
Swimmer	25	75
Cyclist	40	60
800-metre runner	52	48
Untrained person	55	45
Sprinter and jumper	62	38

Analysis of the average proportions of male athletes

(c) What does 'age-matched' mean? Explain why age matching is important.

_____

_____ 2 marks

(d) Explain in general terms how the proportion of fast- and slow-twitch fibres is related to the nature of an athlete's chosen activity.

_____

_____ 2 marks

(e) What statistical test could you apply to the results to see if they were statistically significant? Explain your choice.

_____

_____

_____ 3 marks

(f) In which type of muscle fibre would you expect to find the highest density of mitochondria? Explain your answer.

_____

_____ 2 marks

Total marks: 14

9

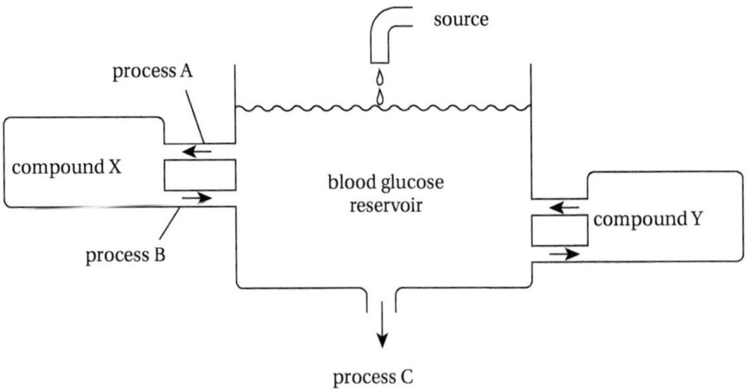

Fig E7
Blood glucose schematic diagram

(a) Compound X (Fig E7) is a carbohydrate, compound Y is not. Name both compounds.

_____

_____ 2 marks

(b) Name the main source of blood glucose.

_____ 1 mark

(c) Name the processes A, B and C.

_____

_____

_____ 3 marks

(d) Which process would be stimulated by insulin?

_____ 1 mark

(e) Which process would be stimulated by glucagon?

_____ 1 mark

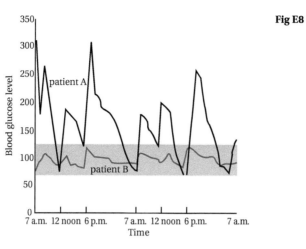

Fig E8

The graph (Fig E8) shows the blood glucose levels of two individuals over a two-day period.

(f) Suggest what is represented by the yellow shaded area.

_____ 1 mark

(g) Identify which patient is the diabetic. Explain your choice.

_____ 1 mark

(h) Describe how the body detects and responds to a rise in blood glucose levels.

_____

_____

_____

_____

_____ 5 marks

Total marks: 15

10 (a) Cattle spread generous amounts of dung (faeces) onto grassland. Explain how the nitrogen in the protein in the dung becomes available to the grass.

_____

_____

_____

_____

_____

_____ 6 marks

(b) Outline the process of eutrophication.

_____

_____

_____

_____

_____ 5 marks

Total marks: 11

11 The diagram below (Fig E9) shows a chloroplast.

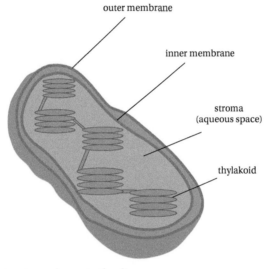

Fig E9

outer membrane

inner membrane

stroma
(aqueous space)

thylakoid

(a) Which one of the structures shown in the diagram:

   (i) … is the site of the light-dependent reactions?

   _____ 1 mark

   (ii) … is the site of the light-independent reactions?

   _____ 1 mark

The graph (Fig E10) shows the effect of light intensity on the rate of photosynthesis.

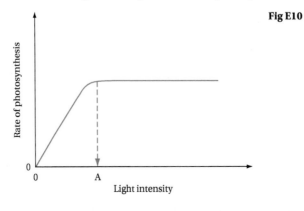

Fig E10

(b) Describe and explain the shape of the curve.

_____

_____

_____ 3 marks

Total marks: 5

12 Match each word with its correct definition.

(a) Glycolysis	(i)	Produces sugar from CO_2
(b) Chlorophyll	(ii)	Energy currency of the cell
(c) Respiration	(iii)	Reduced co-enzyme, electron-carrying molecule
(d) Calvin cycle	(iv)	Breakdown of glucose to pyruvate
(e) NADH	(v)	Produces ATP, NADPH and oxygen
(f) Krebs cycle	(vi)	Central 5-carbon compound in Calvin cycle
(g) Electron transfer chain	(vii)	Takes place on inner mitochondrial membrane
(h) Light-dependent reaction	(viii)	Converts a derivative of pyruvate to CO_2
(i) ATP	(ix)	Emits excited electrons
(j) RuBP	(x)	Oxidation of sugars to produce ATP

Total marks: 10

13 (a) Fill in the table with a tick if the statement is true.

	ATP is made by substrate level phosphorylation	Carbon dioxide is made	Reduced coenzyme is made
Glycolysis			
Link reaction			
Krebs cycle			
Electron transfer chain			

3 marks

Proton pumps are proteins that can be found in the inner mitochondrial membrane and in the thylakoid membranes of chloroplasts.

(b) Explain the importance of proton pumps in the production of ATP.

_____

_____

_____ 3 marks

Total marks: 6

14 (a) Name **two** biologically important organic molecules that contain phosphorus.

_____

_____ 2 marks

(b) In what form do plants absorb phosphorus?

_____ 1 mark

(c) Explain how the absorbed phosphorus travels from the roots to the leaves.

_____

_____ 2 marks

A mycorrhiza is a fungus that grows in and around the roots of some plants. Scientists carried out an investigation into the effect of mycorrhizae on the growth of potato plants. They wanted to find out if growing a crop with a mycorrhiza could result in a reduction in the need for fertiliser.

The scientists chose a phosphorus-based fertiliser. The researchers firstly looked to see if there was a correlation between the concentration of fertiliser applied, and the success of colonisation with mycorrhizae. They added fungal spores to potato plants and grew them in a range of different concentrations of fertiliser. After a set time, they looked to see if the fungus had established itself around the potato roots. Their results are shown in the table below.

Strength of fertiliser/% of manufacturer's recommendation	0	25	50	75	100
Percentage of potato roots colonised with mycorrhiza	4.4	25.7	18.9	14.7	13.1

Table 1

(d) State **three** variables that would need to be controlled in this investigation.

_____

_____

_____ 2 marks

(e) Statistical analysis showed that the results in Table 1 were significant at the $P \geq 0.01$ level. Explain what this means.

_____

_____ 2 marks

Overall, the scientists found that the optimum conditions to increase the yield of potatoes were to add mycorrhizae and fertiliser at 50% of the manufacturer's recommended level.

(f) Outline the significance of this finding to farmers and to the environment.

_____

_____

_____ 3 marks

Total marks: 12

Answers

Question	Answer	Marks
1 (a)	Alternative 1 = taxis (if maggots consistently move to dark with few turns). Alternative 2 = kinesis (if maggots make many more turns).	2
1 (b)	*Any four from*: Use choice chamber. Separate light from dark. Use batch of identical maggots/same species/age. Take one maggot. Count number of turns. Measure time taken to find dark. Repeat.	4
		Total 6
2 (a)	Trophic level X = primary consumers.	1
2 (b)	*Any three from*: A lot of plant material is indigestible. Animals cannot digest cellulose. Animals can only use the energy they absorb. A lot of energy is lost in faeces. A lot of energy is lost as heat to the environment/by-product of respiration. Mice are warm blooded/have a high rate of respiration.	3, one for each
		Total 4
3 (a) (i)	$460 - (230 + 105) = 125$ J	1
3 (a) (ii)	125 as a percentage of $460 = \dfrac{125}{460} \times 100$ $= 27.2\%$	1 1
3 (b)	A large proportion of plant material/cellulose is indigestible. Only the food that is digested and absorbed is available to the caterpillar.	2
3 (c)	*Any two from*: more lost as heat (by-product of respiration); warm blooded/use energy to maintain body temperature; so less energy for new growth.	2, one for each
3 (d)	*Any four from*: Carbon can be found in the organic compounds in the faeces. Carbon can be broken down/hydrolysed/digested by enzymes. It can be released from bacteria/fungi/decomposers in extracellular digestion. Soluble compounds are absorbed into the bodies of decomposers. Carbon dioxide is released into the atmosphere by respiration of decomposers. Carbon dioxide is absorbed by plants; fixed into sugars by photosynthesis.	4, one for each
		Total 11
4 (a)	*Any three from*: Rods are concentrated away from the fovea. Cones are concentrated at the fovea. There are a small number of cones across the retina. There are more rods than cones in total.	3

Question	Answer	Marks
4 (b)	84 000/mm^2 (accept 82–86); 80 000 rods plus about 4 000 cones	1
4 (c)	Cones are found over all of the retina.	1
4 (d)	*Any two from*: Retinal convergence is greater in the cones (or vice-versa). There is more information per unit area from the cones than from the rods. There are more neurones per cone in the optic nerve.	2
		Total 7
5 (a)		3, 1 mark for each neurone in position and correctly labelled
5 (b)	*Any three from*: Reflex arcs have few neurones. They are rapid. They are fixed (one stimulus = one response). They are not under conscious control.	3
5 (c)	The transmitter only is made at the presynaptic membrane. The receptors/receptor proteins only are on the postsynaptic membrane.	2
		Total 8
6 (a)	*Any two from*: All impulses are the same height/size/amplitude. Whatever the size of the stimulus, they are the same. There are no big or small impulses.	2
6 (b)	The more intense the stimulus, the greater the frequency of impulses.	1
6 (c) (i)	*Any two from*: The receptor has adapted. Gel in the Pacinian corpuscle absorbs pressure. The receptor cells not deformed/resumes normal shape.	2
6 (c) (ii)	CNS is not overloaded with irrelevant/old information. This allows the individual to focus on new information.	2
		Total 7
7 (a)	1 = (vi), 2 = (iv), 3 = (i), 4 = (ii), 5 = (viii), 6 = (vii), 7 = (iii), 8 = (v)	2
7 (b)	Mitochondria produce energy/ATP required for: *any two from*: re-synthesis of transmitter substance active transport of calcium ions out of synaptic knob. re-absorption of neurotransmitter (or products of neurotransmitter breakdown).	3

Question	Answer	Marks
7 (c)	Bungarotoxin will cause paralysis/muscles cannot contract. This is because acetylcholine cannot fit into receptors. There is no ion movement/no depolarisation.	2
		Total 7
8 (a)	Contracted sarcomere Z M Z H zone — light band Vital points: sarcomere is shorter; dark bands are wider.	2, 1 mark for each
8 (b)	Calcium diffuses into the muscle fibre across sarcoplasmic reticulum. Binds to/activates troponin. Active troponin moves tropomyosin (so that actin can bind to myosin).	3
8 (c)	*Any two from:* 'Age-matched' means that the men in the sample were of similar age/range of ages. A control is an important variable. It makes comparison valid.	2
8 (d)	Longer events/stamina events require slow-twitch fibres. Short/power events require fast-twitch fibres.	2
8 (e)	Chi squared is the statistical test to apply to the results. This test is used to see if there was a *significant* difference between the observed results and those you would expect by chance/if there was no correlation.	3
8 (f)	There are more mitochondria in slow-twitch fibres. This is because they get the most ATP from *aerobic* respiration.	2
		Total 14
9 (a)	X = glycogen Y = lipid/triglyceride	2, 1 for each
9 (b)	The main source of blood glucose is from digestion/absorption of carbohydrate.	1
9 (c)	A = glycogenesis B = glycogenolysis C = respiration	3, 1 for each
9 (d)	Process B is stimulated by glucagon.	1
9 (e)	Process A is stimulated by insulin.	1
9 (f)	It represents normal range of blood glucose levels (*accept: no symptoms*).	1
9 (g)	Patient A; he or she cannot control blood glucose within normal limits.	1

Question	Answer	Marks
9 (h)	*Any five from*: Rise is detected by the β cells. The β cells secrete insulin. Insulin travels in blood. Target cells are affected, mainly in the liver. Insulin fits into specific protein receptors. This stimulates extra glucose channels to open. Glucose leaves the blood and enters the cells. Insulin activates enzyme pathways. These pathways metabolise glucose.	5
		Total 15
10 (a)	*Any six from*: dung/faecal matter broken down by saprobiotic (saprophytic) decay; bacteria and fungi synthesise and secrete enzymes; proteins hydrolysed into amino acids; process of ammonification; amino acids broken down to release ammonium salts; process of nitrification; changes ammonium into nitrite; the nitrite into nitrate; nitrate is soluble; can be absorbed by plants.	6, one for each
10 (b)	*Any five from*: waterways become over-fertile; due to leaching of minerals (nitrate, phosphate, etc.) from agricultural land; causes algal bloom; algae die/decay; high bacterial population uses most of the available oxygen; normal clean water/high oxygen organisms cannot survive; high BOD (biochemical oxygen demand) value.	5, one for each
		Total 11
11 (a) (i)	Thylakoid is site of light-dependent reactions.	1
11 (a) (ii)	Stroma is site of light-independent reactions.	1
11 (b)	*Any three from*: As light intensity increases so does rate of photosynthesis. Light is the limiting factor. At A some other factor is limiting. For example, carbon dioxide levels may be limiting.	3, one for each
		Total 5
12 (a)	(iv)	1
12 (b)	(ix)	1
12 (c)	(x)	1
12 (d)	(i)	1
12 (e)	(iii)	1
12 (f)	(viii)	1
12 (g)	(vii)	1
12 (h)	(v)	1
12 (i)	(ii)	1
12 (j)	(vi)	1
		Total 10

Question	Answer	Marks
13 (a)		3, 1 for each correct column

	ATP is made by substrate level phosphorylation	Carbon dioxide is made	Reduced coenzyme is made
Glycolysis	✓		✓
Link reaction		✓	✓
Krebs cycle	✓	✓	✓
Electron transfer chain			

Question	Answer	Marks
13 (b)	Creates a concentration gradient or (better answer) an electrochemical gradient. $H+$ ions/protons flow through/drive the ATP synthase enzyme. Which makes ATP from ADP and Pi.	3
		Total 6
14 (a)	*Any two from:* DNA, RNA (accept 'nucleic acids'), ATP, phospholipids	2
14 (b)	Phosphate ions/PO_4^- ions	1
14 (c)	*Any two from:* In the transpiration stream. In the xylem vessels. Due to the cohesion tension hypothesis. Due to evaporation from the leaves.	2
14 (d)	*Any three from:* Same number of spores; Spores from same species; Same variety of potato; Same amount of water; Same amount of light; Same time/duration of trial period.	1 mark for two correct, 2 marks for all three
14 (e)	*Any two from:* The probability that the results are due to chance is equal to or less than 1% so the results are significant.	2
14 (f)	*Any three from:* Reduced cost of fertiliser Additional cost of adding spores Less change of osmotic damage to fungus/potato crop Less leaching Reduced chance of eutrophication.	3
		Total 12

Glossary

Absolute refractory period	See **refractory period**.
Acetate	A 2-carbon molecule produced by the **link reaction** (the oxidation of pyruvate) in aerobic respiration. Combines with **co-enzyme A** to form **acetyl co-enzyme A**. Acetate is basically what is left of the glucose after glycolysis and the **link reaction**.
Acetyl co-enzyme A (acetyl CoA)	Compound that enters the **Krebs cycle**. Co-enzyme A is a carrier molecule that picks up the acetate from the link reaction and delivers it to the Krebs cycle.
Acetylcholine (Ach)	Transmitter substance secreted from the synapses of many nerves, including most of the peripheral nervous system, and the parasympathetic nervous system (PSNS).
Acetylcholincsterase	Enzyme found in the synaptic cleft of cholinergic nerves, where it breaks down acetylcholine, preventing over-stimulation.
Actin	Protein involved in muscular contraction. See also **myosin**.
Action potential	A nerve impulse, a wave of depolarisation that spreads along the axon.
Active transport	Transport across a membrane against a concentration gradient. Requires energy from the cell (ATP).
Adenyl cyclase	Vital enzyme in mechanism of hormone action. Basic sequence of events: Hormone fits into receptor on cell surface membrane → adenyl cyclase activated → second messenger activated → enzymes in cell activated or deactivated.
Aerobic respiration	Respiration that uses oxygen. Results in the complete oxidation of the substrate which produces a lot more ATP than anaerobic respiration. Takes place in the mitochondria. Compare with **anaerobic respiration**.
Ammonification	Vital step in the nitrogen cycle. Process of decay in which proteins and amino acids are broken down by bacteria and fungi to release ammonium salts. Also called **saprobiotic nutrition**. Usually followed by nitrification in the nitrogen cycle.
Anaerobic respiration	Respiration without oxygen. Incomplete oxidation of the substrate (usually glucose) yields a small amount of ATP and an intermediate substance – pyruvate – that is converted into lactate or carbon dioxide/ethanol, depending on the organism. Compare with **aerobic respiration**. Pyruvate is always converted in order to re-synthesise NAD+, so that glycolysis can continue.
Antagonistic	Having an opposing effect. Can apply to muscles, nerves or hormones.
Antidiuretic hormone (ADH)	A peptide hormone produced by the hypothalamus but secreted from the posterior lobe of the pituitary gland; it is a vital part of the negative feedback process that controls the water potential of the blood and body fluids.
Aquaporins	Membrane proteins that act as water channels. Their function is to allow water to flow more quickly through a membrane than would be possible by simple diffusion through the phospholipids. Aquaporins in the DCT and collecting duct of the kidney tubule are under control of the hormone ADH.
Ascending limb	The far part of the loop of Henlé, which leads into the distal convoluted tubule.

ATP	Adenosine triphosphate. Compound that acts as immediate energy source for metabolic reactions. **Respiration** makes ATP from ADP and phosphate; many other processes use ATP, such as muscular contraction, active transport.
Atrioventricular node (AVN)	Part of the conducting pathway of the heart. The AVN picks up the signal from the sinoatrial node (SAN), and delays it (allowing ventricles to fill) before passing it down into the bundle of His.
Autonomic nervous system (ANS)	The system that controls activities that are involuntary, and over which we don't normally have conscious control, including heart rate.
Autotroph	Organism that makes its own food using an external energy source – usually sunlight – and a simple inorganic supply of carbon, usually carbon dioxide. All producers are autotrophs. See **chemoautotroph and photoautotroph.**
Auxin	A plant growth regulator. Often called a plant hormone.
Axon	Long 'thread' that carries impulses from the cell body of a nerve cell to other cells.
Baroreceptor	Receptor cells located in the blood vessels that are sensitive to changes in blood pressure.
Basement membrane	A thin membrane that separates an epithelium from underlying tissue, such as between the endothelium and podocytes in the renal capsule.
Biomass	The mass of living material. Usually applies to the mass of a particular population or trophic level, for example, the mass of all the grass in an ecosystem, but can apply to mass per unit area (such as m^2).
Biotic factor	Environmental factor caused by other organisms, such as food supply, **predation** or disease. Contrast with **abiotic factor**.
Blind spot	Point on the retina where the optic nerve joins. Has no rods or cones so nothing is perceived in that area.
Bowman's capsule	The first region of the kidney nephron. A wine-glass-shaped structure that contains the glomerulus and is the site of filtrate formation.
Bundle of His	Part of the conducting pathway of the heart: a bundle of specialised heart muscle fibres (not nerves) that transmits the impulse from the AVN to the Purkynje fibres.
Calvin cycle	Series of reactions that make up the **light-independent reaction** of photosynthesis. Essentially involves the use of ATP and NADPH to reduce carbon dioxide into glucose.
Cardiac muscle	Muscle that makes up the wall of the heart; produces heartbeat.
Cardiovascular centre	Region in the medulla oblongata in the brain that controls heart rate.
Cell body	The portion of a nerve cell that contains the nucleus and other organelles (such as mitochondria) but does not include the dendrites or axon.
Central nervous system (CNS)	The brain and spinal cord.
Chemiosmosis	The movement of protons through a membrane, down their electrochemical gradient.
Chemoautotroph	Organism that makes its own organic compounds using energy from chemical reactions (usually oxidation). These are all bacteria and nitrifying bacteria are common examples. Compare with **photoautotrophs**.

Chemoreceptor	Receptor cell sensitive to chemical change. For example, the carotid body in the neck contains chemoreceptors sensitive to carbon dioxide levels in blood plasma.
Chlorophyll	Green pigment with a central role in photosynthesis. There are several different pigments that absorb different wavelengths of light, but all essentially absorb light and emit high-energy electrons.
Chloroplast	Organelle of photosynthesis. Contains chlorophyll molecules housed on flat discs (**thylakoids**) piled up into **grana**.
Choice chamber	Apparatus that provides different environmental conditions and can be used to investigate the response of woodlice or other small invertebrates to an environmental stimulus.
Cholinergic synapse	Synapse that secretes acetylcholine (Ach).
Co-enzyme	A general term for any molecule which is needed in order for an enzyme to function. The co-enzymes in respiration and photosynthesis are specifically electron carriers: they become reduced as the substrate is oxidised. The co-enzyme NAD^+ is reduced to become NADH. The co-enzyme $FADH^+$ is reduced to become $FADH_2$. The co-enzyme $NADP^+$ is reduced to become NADPH.
Co-enzyme A (CoA)	In aerobic respiration, compound that combines with **acetate** to form **acetyl co-enzyme A** (**CoA**). CoA combines with the acetate formed in the **link reaction** and transfers it into the **Krebs cycle**.
Collecting duct	The final region of the kidney nephron where selective reabsorption of water takes place; the remaining urine travels down the ureter to the bladder.
Cone cells	Cone-shaped light-sensitive cells in retina. Cones have high visual acuity but low sensitivity to light levels.
Consumer	Organism that cannot make its own organic molecules, and so must obtain them ready-made from other organisms. Animals, fungi and most bacteria are consumers. Contrast with **producer**.
Cristae	Folds in the inner membrane of a mitochondrion; site of the electron transport system.
Cyclic AMP	Second messenger in hormone action. When a hormone fits into a receptor site on the cell membrane, the enzyme **adenyl cyclase** is activated, turning ATP into cyclic AMP.
Cytosol	The fluid part of the cytoplasm; the liquid between the organelles.
Dehydrogenase	An enzyme that catalyses the removal of hydrogen from a substrate to an electron acceptor, such as NADP.
Dendrites	Branched extensions of a nerve cell, along which impulses received from other neurons are passed to the cell body.
Denitrification	In the nitrogen cycle, a bacterial process that converts soluble nitrate into nitrogen gas (N_2), thereby losing it from the ecosystem. Tends to occur in anaerobic conditions, such as waterlogged soil.
Denitrifying bacteria	Bacteria responsible for **denitrification**.
Depolarisation	A sudden change in the polarity of a cell's membrane potential, making the inside of the cell less negative for a very brief time.
Descending limb	The first part of the loop of Henlé.

Detritus	Rotting organic matter such as dead leaves, wood, animal bodies and faeces.
Distal convoluted tubule	The far, twisted part of the kidney nephron between the loop of Henlé and the collecting duct. The permeability of the tubule is under the influence of the hormone ADH. When the body needs to conserve water, ADH activates membrane proteins called aquaporins, which make the tubule wall more permeable to water. As a result, more water leaves the filtrate and re-enters the blood.
Ecosystem	Natural unit such as a lake, woodland, coral reef, etc. that contains many different species together with the non-living components.
Effector	An organ or cell that carries out a response to a nerve impulse.
Electron transfer chain	The final stage of aerobic respiration in which electrons are transported along a series of proteins on the inner mitochondrial membrane. The resulting redox reactions release energy that is used to pump protons (H^+ ions) into the outer mitochondrial membrane. Diffusion of protons back into the matrix through channels in ATP synthase molecules powers ATP synthesis. Electron transfer chains also play an important role in the light-dependent reaction of photosynthesis.
Endothelium	A layer of cells that forms the lining of organs and cavities of the body.
EPSP	Excitatory postsynaptic potential – a charge that builds up in a neurone after synaptic transmission. If the EPSP reaches a threshold, an impulse is created.
Ethanol	Ethyl alcohol, C_2H_5OH. It makes you drunk.
Eutrophication	In ecology, a situation where a waterway is over-fertile due to excess fertiliser. Main stages: Algal bloom → bacterial bloom → oxygen shortage.
Extracellular digestion	Mode of nutrition in which organisms (bacteria or fungi) synthesise and release enzymes that digest the surrounding organic material. The organisms then absorb the soluble products. Basically, this is why things rot.
Fast-twitch muscle fibres	A type of skeletal muscle fibre that contracts quickly.
Filtrate	Fluid that results from filtration.
Fovea	Region of the retina where cones are concentrated, allowing us to see in detail and in colour.
Generator potential	The charge built up when sodium ions flood into a receptor cell.
Glomerulus	A knot of capillaries found in the Bowman's capsule. Blood entering the glomerulus is subjected to ultrafiltration: the process that makes the filtrate.
Glomerular filtrate	Fluid that is formed by ultrafiltration in the Bowman's capsule of the nephron. The filtrate has a similar composition to tissue fluid, i.e. blood plasma without the large proteins.
Glucagon	Hormone, secreted by the α cells in the **islets of Langerhans** of the pancreas, in response to low blood glucose levels. Antagonistic hormone to insulin.
Gluconeogenesis	The production of new glucose from non-carbohydrate sources (i.e. protein or lipid, but not glycogen). This happens during fasting/dieting/starvation, when glucose and glycogen levels are low.
Glycerate 3-phosphate (GP or G3P)	A 3-carbon compound, it is the first sugar made in the light-independent reaction of photosynthesis, sometimes referred to as GALP – glyceraldehyde phosphate.
Glycogen	The main storage carbohydrate in animals. A highly branched polymer of glucose, so it can be built up and broken down quickly. Stored in many cells, but notably those of the liver and muscles.

Glycogenesis	The production of glycogen by the polymerisation of glucose.
Glycogenolysis	The breakdown of glycogen to release glucose. Stimulated (indirectly) by the hormone glucagon.
Glycolysis	The first stage of respiration, in which glucose is converted into **pyruvate**. It's a universal process, taking place in the cytoplasm of all cells in all organisms, whether anaerobic or aerobic. Makes 2 ATP and 2 NADH molecules per glucose molecule.
Granum	A pile of **thylakoids** in a **chloroplast**. Site of chlorophyll and therefore of the light-dependent reaction in photosynthesis.
Gravitropism	Directional growth of a plant in response to the stimulus of gravity, caused by the movement of IAA to the underside of a stem or seedling so there is uneven growth.
Gross primary production (GPP)	The rate at which the producers in an ecosystem make biomass (organic material such as sugars, starches and cellulose) during photosynthesis. See also **net primary production** (**NPP**).
Homeostasis	The ability of an organism to maintain its internal conditions within certain limits, for example, pH of blood, body temperature and blood glucose levels.
Hormone	Chemical, secreted by an endocrine gland, that has an effect on a target organ or cell.
Humus	Rotting organic matter in soil – a sticky mass of dead plants, dead animals and faeces. Humus is vital to soil because it improves texture and allows it to hold more water. Saprobionts act on humus to release the nutrients – such as nitrate and phosphate – that plants need to grow.
Hypothalamus	Vital part of brain. Sensitive to many different internal and external stimuli. Controls the secretions of the pituitary gland and therefore of the whole endocrine system.
Indoleacetic acid (IAA)	The main auxin (plant growth regulator) involved in tropisms.
Insulin	Hormone made by β cells in **islets of Langerhans**. Works by stimulating cells to open extra glucose channels in cell membranes, so that glucose can leave the blood and enter cells, where it can be metabolised.
Iodopsin	Light-sensitive pigment found only in the cone cells on the **retina**.
IPSP	Inhibitory postsynaptic potential; a charge that builds up in the postsynaptic membrane of inhibitory synapses. IPSPs exist to inhibit action potential in particular neurones. See **EPSP**.
Islets of Langerhans	Patches of endocrine (hormone-producing) tissue in the pancreas. Contain α and β cells that secrete **glucagon** and **insulin**, respectively.
Kinesis	Simple behavioural response in animals, in which a stimulus leads to a non-directional response; for example, woodlice responding to light. See also **taxis**.
Krebs cycle	Stage in aerobic respiration that takes place in the matrix of a mitochondrion. Begins with **acetyl co-enzyme A** and produces reduced co-enzymes (NADH and $FADH_2$), ATP, and CO_2 as a by-product.
Lactate	A 3-carbon molecule produced in **anaerobic respiration** in various organisms. Builds up during muscle fatigue. Lactate is lactic acid in solution.

Leaching	When mineral ions (nitrate, phosphate, etc.) are washed out of soil, such as when rainfall washes ions away from fertilised farmland and into waterways, leading to eutrophication.
Legume	Plant that has root nodules containing **nitrogen-fixing bacteria**, which convert N_2 gas into nitrate. Includes peas, beans, lentils, clover and peanuts.
Light-dependent reaction	First stage of photosynthesis – chlorophyll absorbs light and emits two high-energy 'excited' electrons. ATP and NADPH are the vital products of the light reaction. Takes place on the thylakoids.
Light-independent reaction	Second stage of photosynthesis in which carbon dioxide is used to make sugar, via the reactions of the **Calvin cycle**. Happens in the **stroma** (fluid) of chloroplasts.
Limiting factor	The factor that is in short supply. If supply is increased, the rate of the process increases too. Light is a common limiting factor for photosynthesis.
Link reaction	In respiration, stage that links glycolysis to the Krebs cycle. Pyruvate is converted into acetate, which is picked up by **co-enzyme A** to become **acetyl co-enzyme A**. Also known as pyruvate oxidation.
Loop of Henlé	The part of a kidney tubule which forms a long loop in the central part of the kidney. Its function is to create a region of high sodium chloride concentration, and hence low water potential, deep in the medulla of the kidney.
Matrix	Fluid in the centre of mitochondria. Site of the link reaction and the **Krebs cycle**.
Mitochondrion	Organelle found in most eukaryote cells. Site of **aerobic respiration**.
Motor neurone	A neurone that carries impulses from the CNS to an effector (muscle or gland).
Mutualism	An association between two organisms where both species benefit. Old name: symbiosis. Examples include lichens (algae inside fungi), corals (algae inside animals) and legumes (nitrogen-fixing bacteria in plant roots).
Mycorrhizae	A fungus that grows in and around the roots of most plants, which benefits the plants by facilitating the uptake of inorganic ions.
Myofibrils	Thin filaments (myofilaments) in muscles; in bundles, which bring about contraction.
Myogenic	Originating from the muscle. Refers to the fact that cardiac muscle cells, and therefore the heart as a whole, beats on its own rather than needing nervous stimulation.
Myosin	Protein involved in muscular contraction. See **actin**.
NAD	Co-enzyme that plays a central part in respiration. NAD picks up an electron to become reduced NAD, also called NADH.
NADP	Co-enzyme that plays a central part in photosynthesis. NADP picks up an electron to become reduced NAD, also called NADPH.
Negative feedback	A control system for stability. A change is detected and initiates a corrective mechanism to reverse the change. Contrast with **positive feedback**.
Nephron	Another term for a tubule in the kidney, where water and useful substances are reabsorbed into the blood.
Nerve impulse	Electrical signals transmitted along axons and dendrites.

Net primary production (NPP)	The rate of accumulation of biomass by photosynthesis after respiration has been taken into account. NPP = GPP – respiration.
Neuromuscular junction	A type of synapse that is the junction between a motor neurone and a muscle cell.
Neurone	A specialised nerve cell that can transmit impulses.
Nitrification	Vital two-stage process in the nitrogen cycle. Ammonium salts are converted first into nitrite, then into nitrate.
Nitrifying bacteria	Bacteria that carry out nitrification. See **nitrogen cycle.**
Nitrogen cycle	Cycle of reactions that re-uses nitrogen. Plants absorb nitrate and use it to make proteins and nucleic acids. In this form nitrogen passes up the food chain until it is broken down into nitrate again by the action of saprobionts and **nitrifying bacteria**.
Nitrogen fixation	Process in which nitrogen gas is converted, via ammonia (NH_3), into soluble nitrate so that it is available to organisms. Can happen in the atmosphere during electrical storms but is more commonly done by bacteria living free in soil/water or inside plant roots (see **legumes**).
Nitrogenase	Enzyme found in nitrogen-fixing bacteria that converts nitrogen gas into ammonia, which can then be converted into nitrate.
Nitrogen-fixing bacteria	Bacteria that carry out nitrogen fixation. See **Rhizobium.**
Optic nerve	Carries nerve impulses from the retina to the brain.
Osmoreceptor cells	Cells in the hypothalamus that monitor the concentration of solutes in the blood.
Osmoregulation	The control of water potential of body fluids, including blood.
Oxidation	In oxidation reactions, electrons are removed from a substance.
Oxidative phosphorylation	ATP made by the electron transport chain. In respiration there are two basic methods of making ATP – the other being **substrate level phosphorylation**. Oxidative phosphorylation yields far more ATP per glucose molecule (over 30 compared with just four).
Pacinian corpuscle	Touch receptor in the skin. Detects heavy pressure and vibration.
Parasympathetic nervous system (PSNS)	One division of the autonomic nervous system. Generally, stimulation of parasympathetic nerves will return the body to normal, for example, slowing down the heart. See also **sympathetic nervous system** (SNS).
Phosphocreatine	A compound which acts as an energy store in muscles and can be broken down to transfer a phosphate group to ADP to form ATP without respiration.
Phosphorus cycle	The movement of phosphorus through the lithosphere, hydrosphere, and biosphere; saprophytic decay releases phosphate ions, which can be absorbed by plants and used to make vital phosphorus-containing compounds such as ATP and DNA.
Phosphorylation	This simply means adding a phosphate (PO_4^-) ion. The phosphorylation of glucose is the important first step in glycolysis. ATP is made by phosphorylation, when a phosphate group is added to ADP.
Photoautotroph	Organism that makes organic compounds using energy from sunlight; i.e. an organism that photosynthesises. Compare with **chemoautotroph**.
Photoionisation	The ionisation process by which a molecule of chlorophyll emits two high-energy electrons when it absorbs light.

Photolysis	In photosynthesis, the splitting of water to provide replacement electrons for those lost by chlorophyll in the light-dependent reaction. Vitally, oxygen is a by-product.
Photophosphorylation	The production of ATP during the light-dependent reaction of photosynthesis.
Photosynthesis	Series of reactions in which sunlight energy is used to synthesise organic compounds such as sugars. Vital process which is virtually the only route of energy into most ecosystems. Makes all the food on the planet, removes carbon dioxide and produces oxygen.
Phototropism	Directional growth of a plant in response to the stimulus of light, caused by the movement of IAA to cells on the shaded side of a shoot so there is uneven growth.
Pituitary gland	A key endocrine gland that controls the activities of many other endocrine glands.
Podocytes	Cells in the Bowman's capsule in the kidneys that wrap around capillaries of the glomerulus.
Positive feedback	A control mechanism in which change leads to more change.
Producer	Organism that can photosynthesise. They produce organic compounds such as sugars from inorganic compounds, notably carbon dioxide and water. Plants, algae and photosynthetic bacteria are all producers.
Proximal convoluted tubule	The first, twisted part of the kidney nephron. Responsible for a lot of the reabsorption of filtrate back into the blood.
Purkynje fibres	specialised cardiac muscle fibres that initiate contraction of the ventricles. This contraction begins at the apex so that blood is forced up into the arteries.
Pyruvate	A 3-carbon compound produced in glycolysis from the splitting of glucose. One glucose molecule produces two pyruvate molecules.
Receptor	A cell that can detect a particular **stimulus**. Receptors are able to transduce the energy in the stimulus into a nervous impulse.
Redox reaction	A reaction in which one substance is reduced and one substance is oxidised.
Reduced NAD	Electron-carrying co-enzyme with a vital role in respiration. Co-enzyme, often written as NAD^+, picks up an electron to become reduced co-enzyme, often written as NADH.
Reduction	In reduction reactions, substances gain electrons.
Reflex	Simple coordinated response that is generally fixed. One stimulus leads to a particular response.
Reflex arc	The pathway taken by impulses in a reflex. Generally involves very few neurones; sensory neurones, **relay neurones** (in the CNS) and motor neurones.
Refractory period	'Recovery period'. The time after a nerve impulse has passed when it is impossible (absolute refractory period) or more difficult (relative refractory period) to generate another impulse. Ensures that impulses are discrete, i.e. do not blend.
Relative refractory period	See **refractory period**.
Repolarisation	Restoring the resting potential in a nerve cell after depolarization.
Relay neurone	Neurone in the spinal cord that directly connects sensory and motor neurones, thus completing the fastest possible circuit in a **reflex arc**.

Respiration	Process that releases energy in organic molecules and transfers it to **ATP** so the cell/organism has instant energy available. Universal process, one of the seven signs of life.
Resting potential	A state of readiness in neurones. An electrical charge across the axon membrane, created by an unequal distribution of ions, where the outside is positive relative to the inside. See also **action potential**.
Retina	Layer on the back of the eye that contains the rods and cones; photosensitive receptors.
Retinal convergence	Arrangement of neurones in the retina. Many rod cells converge into one sensory neurone in the optic nerve. There is much less convergence from the cone cells. Thus rods are more sensitive because they summate, but cones supply more detail per unit area of retina, resulting in much higher visual acuity.
R_f value	A measurement used to identify the substances in a mixture, following paper chromatography. The R_f value is worked out as: $$\frac{\text{distance travelled by centre of pigment spot from origin}}{\text{distance travelled by solvent front from origin.}}$$ Each substance has a particular R_f value in any given solvent.
Rhizobium	Genus of **nitrogen-fixing bacteria** found in the root nodules of legumes. An example of a mutualism, both bacteria and plants benefit from this association. **Rhizobium** cannot fix nitrogen outside the plant.
Rhodopsin	Light-sensitive pigment found in rod cells. Made from retinine (made from vitamin A) and opsin, a protein.
Ribulose bisphosphate (RuBP)	Ribulose bisphosphate. Vital 5-carbon compound in the light-independent reaction in photosynthesis.
Rod cells	Rod-shaped light-sensitive cells in the retina, not sensitive to colour. Low visual acuity but high sensitivity to light levels.
Rubisco	Ribulose-1,5-bisphosphate carboxylase. Enzyme that catalyses the reaction between RuBP and carbon dioxide in the light-independent reaction (Calvin cycle) of photosynthesis. Thought to be the most abundant protein on Earth.
Saltatory conduction	Type of rapid conduction seen in myelinated nerves, where the impulse 'jumps' from node (of Ranvier) to node.
Saprobiont	Preferred name for **saprophyte**. A decomposer that breaks down dead organic matter by extracellular digestion. Mainly bacteria or fungi, they secrete enzymes and absorb the soluble products of digestion.
Saprobiotic nutrition	name for saprophytic decay, a process in which bacteria and fungi break down dead organic matter by extracellular digestion.
Saprophyte	Old name for **saprobiont**.
Sarcomere	In skeletal muscle, one repeated pattern of actin and myosin fibres. When actin and myosin slide over each other, the sarcomeres shorten and the muscle contracts.
Sarcoplasmic reticulum	Modified endoplasmic reticulum seen in muscle fibres. Motor impulses spread from neuromuscular junction along the sarcoplasmic reticulum, altering the permeability of the membrane to calcium. The influx of calcium initiates contraction.
Selective reabsorption	Taking back useful substances into the blood, from the fluid inside a nephron.

Sensory neurone	Neurones that pass from receptors to the CNS, bringing sensory information about the internal and external environment.
Sino-atrial node (SAN)	The heart's pacemaker. Situated in the wall of the left atrium, the SAN generates the impulse that stimulates the atria and, after a delay, the ventricles, to contract. Modified by two nerves from the brain.
Skeletal muscle	Muscles attached to bone, that produce movement and maintain posture.
Slow-twitch muscle fibres	A type of skeletal muscle fibre that contracts slowly.
Smooth muscle	Muscle tissue in which the contractile fibrils are not highly ordered, occurring in the gut and other internal organs and not under voluntary control.
Spatial summation	Where two or more impulses, separated in space, combine to trigger an action potential.
Specific heat capacity	The amount of energy needed to change the temperature of 1 kg of a substance by 1°C.
Stimulus	A change in the environment that can be detected by a **receptor**.
Stroma	The fluid part of a chloroplast. Contains all the enzymes and intermediates for the **light-independent reaction** in photosynthesis.
Substrate level phosphorylation	ATP produced from glycolysis and the Krebs cycle, a total of four molecules per glucose. Contrast with ATP made from **oxidative phosphorylation**, which is ATP generated by the electron transport system (over 30 molecules in total).
Sympathetic nervous system (SNS)	Part of the autonomic nervous system, along with the **parasympathetic nervous system** (*PSNS*).
Synapse	A junction between two neurones. Synapses allow the selection of different neural pathways – the underlying process behind all movement, thought and coordination.
Taxis	Simple behavioural response in which an organism moves towards or away from a directional stimulus. See also **kinesis**.
Temporal summation	Where two or more impulses arrive in quick succession to trigger an action potential.
Thylakoid	Flat disc-shaped membrane that houses the **chlorophyll** inside a **chloroplast**. A pile of thylakoids forms one **granum**.
Transmitter substance	Substance secreted by synapses. Transmitters such as **acetylcholine** (*Ach*) are released from vesicles in the presynaptic membrane.
Triose phosphate (TP)	A 3-carbon sugar that is the first carbohydrate produced in the light-independent reaction of photosynthesis (also known as the Calvin cycle).
Trophic level	A 'feeding' level in the food web. The first trophic level usually consists of producers, though *detritivores* can also support a food web. The next trophic level is the primary *consumers* (usually herbivores), then secondary consumers (carnivores) and sometimes tertiary consumers or even higher. Some animals are omnivorous, for example, rats, pigs and monkeys. They have a very varied diet and so can occupy more than one trophic level.
Tropism	A growth response seen in plants. A negative phototropism is growth away from light, while a positive geotropism would be growth towards gravity.
Tropomyosin	Protein involved in muscular contraction. A long, thin, spiral protein that winds around actin, covering the myosin binding sites.

Troponin	Protein involved in muscular contraction. Troponin is activated by calcium ions. When activated, it binds to tropomyosin, moving it out of the way and allowing myosin to bind to actin.
Ultrafiltration	Filtration under pressure. Occurs when hydrostatic pressure forces the smaller components of blood plasma through a capillary wall. A key process in the formation of tissue fluid, and of the formation of glomerular filtrate in the kidney.
Ureter	One of the tubes that carries urine from the kidneys to the bladder.
Vasa recta	A network of blood capillaries surrounding the loop of Henlé.
Visual acuity	The ability to see in detail. Acuteness or clarity of vision.
Water potential	A measure of the tendency of a cell or solution to gain water by osmosis. Always a negative scale. Pure water has a water potential of zero.

Index

Notes